Akemi's Journal 3

AKEMI TOMODA

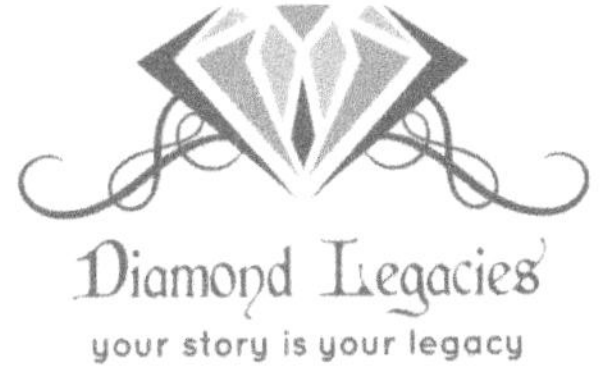

Table of Contents

In Gratitude

I am very thankful that God took me into His family and poured out His love upon me.

When I lost my husband, Ken Tomoda, 20 years ago, I never thought I would be able to survive even for one year by myself. But now already 20 years have passed. God helped me so much. Without His help I could never have made it. I am so thankful for that.

God surrounded me with so many wonderful people and helped me to go through my life.

I am very grateful to Keith Sproule, who offered to check my essays after my wonderful English teacher, Eleanor Sproule, moved to Heaven. He still checks my essays and encourages me to keep on writing.

I am very thankful for my wonderful trustees, Janis Flowers and Gary Brady. They have been helping me for the last 20 years and made my life so safe. Janis calls me often and encourages me in her busy life. Gary still comes and cuts grass so neatly, even though he moved to Guelph.

I am thankful for Rita Gerveis. She has visited me, and we have prayed together in my living room for the last 20 years. I always enjoy our prayer time because God joins us there.

I am thankful for Anita Khan, who helps me a lot. Especially after the coronavirus spread, she takes me out for shopping once a week. She makes my life so safe.

I am thankful for Daniel Hoogsteen and his parents, Doug and Nanette, for their kind help in my life. They keep on delivering delicious, cooked food to me.

I am thankful for my sister, Sanae Sakurai, who still calls me often from Japan and encourages me.

I am thankful for Janette Schliephabe, Dianne Schleifer, Ellie Murach, Ann Hanson, and Sharon Yovanovski, who helped me tremendously to live my life and also to continue my journey deep into the heart of God.

I truly thank God who sent me these wonderful people into my life, and also, I thank God who has been with me all the time.

Introduction

I was born in a little village in Japan before World War II. My father was a schoolteacher, and his family believed in Buddhism for many generations, and my mother was a daughter of a Shinto priest. We experienced hardship and food shortage during World War Two, but we managed quite well, and I was a happy child.

After I graduated from teacher's college, I started to suffer from depression. At first it was not a big problem, but it became deeper and deeper, and I did not want to live anymore. I read so many books to find an answer to my problem, but I could not find any. During this time, I came across a tiny book, For Sleepless Nights, written by Carl Hilty. He wrote only about God's love and friendship with Jesus Christ, which I did not understand at all. But one sentence from his book touched my heart deeply. He wrote "if you feel like shooting yourself in the head with a gun, read a Bible instead, and if you want to hang yourself with a rope, go to a church instead." I wanted to be free from depression so badly that I tried it. I started going to a church by riding a bicycle for 15 minutes and taking a train to the next city and walked about 30 minutes, because there wasn't a Christian church in our little village and there were no Christians. After a couple of years struggle, I finally became a Christian in the year of 1965. I was baptized in the name of the Father and the Son and the Holy Spirit, at a little charge in Mihara.

I met Ken Tomoda in the early spring of 1970 in Japan, while he was on vacation from Canada to visit his family. We exchanged many letters, and I decided to come to Canada to marry him in the fall of 1970, and lived in North York for several years, and later moved to Mississauga.

In Canada, I experienced the Toronto Airport Church's revival, and I was touched by the Holy Spirit.

After several years of prayers, my husband became a Christian and we read 2 Bibles together and prayed together. We enjoyed a beautiful time together. In January 2000, my husband invited Jesus into his heart, and his eyes started shining so beautifully. I was so happy to be with him, and only four months later, one beautiful sunny Saturday morning, he passed away suddenly from a massive heart attack.

That moment everything changed. I was overwhelmed by the grief of my husband's death and the worries about my future living in a foreign country without a husband and children. I could not eat anything for 2 1/2 weeks and shed tears every day for more than three months.

I just cried and cried, and one day I said to God with tears, "Lord, I can't live like this. My sorrow is so deep. I haven't touched the bottom of it. All our dreams are shattered, and all our hopes are gone. I can't live like this." Then God spoke to me, "Akemi, my love is bigger than your sorrow. My love is bigger than your shattered dreams and hope." I thought about Jesus' death on the cross for me and for all human beings. Through my deep sorrow I came to know God's huge love for me.

It was very difficult, but I started living by myself one day at a time. It was very hard, and I needed lots of help. I said to God, "Father, I am in the fiery furnace. The fire is burning. Help me! If you fail to help me, I can't survive."

God responded to my request. He helped me so wonderfully well by sending many kind people into my life. Many Christians helped me with prayers and encouragement, and many neighbours helped me in so many ways so that I was able to live without a husband and children.

God also helped me and heals me through writing essays. My English teacher, Eleanor Sproule visited me and taught me English even before my husband's death. After my husband's death, I could not think of anything, so I stopped taking English lessons, but I resumed it after a few months. Every time Eleanore visited me, I presented one essay, and I decided to write about the goodness of God in my life. This helped me to go through the most difficult time in my life. I tried to see something good in my life instead of difficulties. I trained my mind to see something good. I also learned the importance of thanksgiving in my life, because God is bigger than any trouble I face on earth.

God healed me with watercolour painting. My husband loved art so much and he introduced me to art. He took me to New York, Chicago, Buffalo, Ottawa, and Toronto to visit art galleries. After his death, I started taking art classes at Visual Arts Mississauga and found such joy in painting. When I paint, I lose myself completely in painting and nothing bothers me anymore. I thank God for that.

God healed me through gardening. Ken left quite a big garden in my backyard. It was his garden, and I did not touch it at all. But after his sudden death, I had to look after the garden by myself. Right after I watered the garden for the first time, I cried out to God, "Lord help me. I must look after the garden by myself now. Send me someone who can help me to look after the garden."

Then two hours later, Phyllis, a lady who lived on our street, brought a young man to my home, and said, "Akemi, this is Gary." I looked at the tall, handsome man who was silent. Phyllis said again, "Akemi, Gary wants to help you." Then Gary said, "I am your gardener." I cried. Since then, Gary has helped me in the garden and in the house too. He helped me a lot, and I really thanked God for that.

In the year 2001, one Sunday in early summer, I came home from church and opened the living room door to go out into the garden, and God spoke to me, "Thank you for looking after my garden." I was shocked and could not move for a long time. Since then I started calling my backyard 'The Lord's Garden' and I started sensing the peace of God and enjoyed it so much. I also started seeing double rainbows in the garden every time I watered it. I was so excited to see the double rainbows and I thanked God.

Twenty years passed since my husband's death. God has helped me and healed me so wonderfully well. He rescued me from the fiery furnace. He was with me all these years. I wasn't burned by the fire. I did not become angry or a bitter person. I am so thankful for that. I am still writing about the goodness of God in my life and I thank God every time I write.

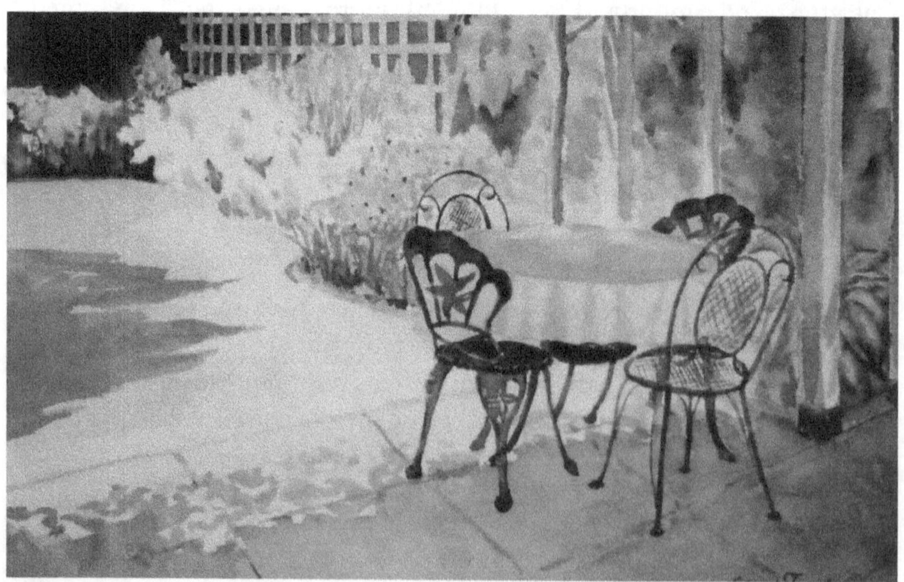

1

I Fixed My Car

The 11th of April was a beautiful day with the sky so blue and the air was warm. This was the first day I wore a spring jacket this year. "Now spring has come! Thank you, Father. I will enjoy this spring in our garden again."

With thanksgiving in my heart, I drove to a medical centre in Meadowvale Town Centre to have a physio treatment for my right shoulder at Lifemark. After I received a gentle treatment from a physiotherapist named Michel, I came out of the building and I drove to Metro, a supermarket very close to the Medical Centre. I found a nice parking spot and parked my car nearly. I was so happy that I could still drive a car and go to many places by myself.

A week ago, Lou Michel called me and wanted to visit me on the 12th of April. Lou was a very good friend of my husband, Ken. While Ken was alive, they attended a men's Bible study together and went to restaurants for lunches often. After Ken's death, Lou helped me a lot. I was so happy to see Lou on the following day. Since I know that Lou loves mocha cappuccino, I went to Metro and bought a box of cappuccino and a little snack and got out of the store and walked to my car. The air was warm and comfortable. I sat on the car seat and turned the key to start the engine, but it did not start. I tried again but it did not work. I tried many times with prayers, but it did not work at all. I knew I had to call C.A.A. I took out my cellphone, but it was completely out of power. I could not use it at all.

I went back to Meadowvale Town Centre to use a public phone, but I realized I did not have enough change. I went to the store and changed a 20-dollar bill into small change.

Finally, I called CAA and talked to a lady about my car's problem.

She asked me so many questions and told me that she would send me a technician in 45 minutes. I was so relieved and thanked God that a helper was coming soon. I wanted to talk to someone about my situation, but I could not call my trustees, because Gary moved far away to Guelph and he was busy, also I knew Janis was very busy nowadays. I decided to call my good friend Rita, and used a public phone again, but Rita wasn't at home.

I came back to my car and sat on the seat. "So, Lord, just you and me now. Please send me a CAA technician quickly and let him find my car easily. Please fix my car nicely," I asked.

I went out and stood close to the Metro building. It was about 3:40, so I had to wait until 4:30, but the air was still warm, and my spring jacket was light. It wasn't raining even though we had so much rain recently. I really thanked God for that. When I got tired standing, I went to my car and sat in the car.

While I was standing, I watched many cars coming into the mall parking lot. I especially watched carefully for white cars, assuming CAA would come with a white car, but many white trucks went to the beer store.

After about 30 minutes, I found a small car with blue letters CAA. I moved to my car quickly and waved my hand. The car came straight to my car. I was so happy to see a young technician come out of the car.

"Hi, thank you for coming. I am Akemi." He shook my hand.

He opened the front of my car and started checking the battery, and said, "Your battery is okay." He also checked his computer and said, "Your battery is only two years old. I will check the starter." He looked for awhile and said, "It's funny I can't find a starter."

I said, "Oh no, that is why I can't start my car."

He said, "No, no you have one. I just can't find it." We both laughed.

Then suddenly someone said from behind me, "Hi Akemi." I looked back and saw my neighbours. The mother and daughter who lived right in front of my house were standing there. I said to Shirley and Tracy, "Hi, good to see you."

"Do you have a problem with your car? What happened?" they asked.

While I was talking to Shirley and Tracy about my problem, the CAA technician found out that the starter wasn't working, and he wanted to call a tow truck to take my car to a dealer. He asked me where I wanted to take my car to be fixed. I told him to take it to Canadian Tire because it is in the same mall.

Tracy said, "We will be with you. We will go to Canadian Tire together and drive you home and when your car is fixed, I will drive you here again."

"Really? Thank you so much." I could not believe what just happened. I really thanked them and thanked God in my heart.

The CAA technician called a tow truck and told me to wait another 30 minutes and he left. Shirley was with me while Tracy went to the shop to do shopping, and we sat in my car and talked. When Tracy came back, Shirley went to do her shopping.

Soon a tow truck came and put my car on the truck and drove to Canadian Tire. Tracy followed the truck, and I registered for a new starter. A young man checked the computer and said, "we have just one starter in the store. Would you like us to install it?"

"Of course, please do. I can't do that."

He told me that it would take about one hour, and he would call me when my car was fixed. Tracy drove me home. I was so thankful for that. I did not have to wait at Canadian Tire another hour.

As soon as I was at home, I charged my cell phone and ate a simple supper. I had to wait about two hours, but Canadian Tire called me, and I called Tracy, and she drove me to Canadian Tire again. As soon as we arrived in front of the garage, I saw my car was in the parking lot. I paid the money for the repair and I got my car key. Everything went well and I was so happy. I thanked Tracy for her kind help. Then she said, "you're welcome, Akemi. I want you to keep our phone number in your wallet and if you need help, call my mother. She will ask someone to help you. Okay?" I really thanked her.

I turned the car key on, and the car started smoothly. I drove home with a big thanksgiving in my heart for sending me wonderful helper at the perfect timing. While I was driving, I was so happy as if I were driving a brand-new car.

2

Lord Increase Your Presence

On the 22nd April, I drove to our church thirty minutes before the service started. I put my Bible and my purse on a chair and went to the back of the auditorium. Actually, it is a gym, because we are using Dolphin Junior High School's gym for our worship gathering. Our worship team was already on the stage and practising worship music. I started praying for the cleaning of the room with the blood of Jesus, and asking God to bless our Sunday service, touching each one of our hearts deeply. I asked God to increase His presence, His anointing, His fire, His healing, and to increase our numbers.

The service started and I went to my chair and started singing worship music. Then suddenly my throat started to choke, and my chest became tight. I had a hard time to breathe. I realized that my throat was reacting towards some perfume or hair spray, so I moved to the very back and stood behind the last row of chairs. I worshipped our God from the back for a while and realized that my throat and breathing was getting easier. I enjoyed praising God, thanked him for changing my life completely. He took me out of the darkness into His light. It was so wonderful to praise him with my brothers and sisters in the Lord!

While I was enjoying worshiping God, one lady came to me and said, "Good morning, Akemi." I said, "Good morning, Shirley," and we hugged each other.

Shirley started coming to our prayer meeting which was held at my house a few weeks ago. She said she had breast cancer and went through surgery and now she is taking treatments. I put my hand over her and prayed over her. While I put my right hand over her breast, I sensed the Holy Spirit went through me thoroughly. I kept on praying.

Then she said to me, "Do I need a baptism?"

"You were baptized, right?" I asked.

Then she said, "Yes, I was baptized, but it was in a Catholic Church."

I did not know what to say about it. I just said "If you need a baptism of the Holy Spirit, I can pray for you. I pray that the Holy Spirit would come into Shirley's life and thanked God for taking her into His family. I sensed strongly the Spirit of God moving in my body again and again, and Shirley's body started reacting to the Spirit. Suddenly Shirley started laughing, and I laughed too. It was such a joy. We jumped and laughed, holding hands together at the back of the church and enjoyed singing worship music together. I really enjoyed it.

Shirley said, "Akemi, I am laughing. I am laughing!"

"Yes, you are, so what?"

"I have never laughed for the last four months. I could not laugh."

"Good for you," I said, and we laughed more together. Everything was so light, and I felt such freedom.

Then Shirley said, "I am so hot. I am so hot." She took off her jacket. She looked at me and said, "I have energy in my body. I have energy. I can run now."

"That's good," I said.

"You know I was so tired when I came to church this morning. Now I can run!"

We thanked God for His kindness towards all His children. Then the worship music ended. Shirley went to sit with her husband, and I went back to my seat. I was able to sit without choking this time. I was so thankful for God to use me for His purpose. I said in my heart, "Thank you, Father. Increase Your presence. Increase your anointing. Increase your fire. Increase your healing and increase the numbers in this church. Your will be done."

The following Sunday, on the 30th April, I went to church thirty minutes earlier as usual, and prayed for our church, cleansing the building, and inviting angels and declared God's blessings over us. I kept on asking God to increase His presence, His anointing, His fire, His healing and our numbers.

When I started asking this prayer about one year ago, we had around sixty to seventy adults in the church, but now we have 150 to 170 people each Sunday and I am so excited about praying for our church. I really enjoy praying for our church and talking to God, expecting His wonderful answers.

On that Sunday, right after the service, while I was preparing to come home, one lady approached me and said, "Are you Akemi?"

"Yes, I am," I said.

Then she said, "I heard that you are praying for this church every Sunday morning."

"Yes, I do," I said, "since I started coming to this church, I come thirty minutes early and pray for the church. I asked Pastor James about it and I got permission for this."

I told her that we are using the junior high school gym as a church and there are lots of students coming here with unclean spirits.

Then she said, "Oh good! Won't you join us to pray for our church? We like to pray every Sunday morning. Please join us at 10 o'clock from next Sunday."

"I will. I am happy to do that. Thank you for inviting me," I said.

I learned the lady's name is Selina and we prayed a short prayer together and left the church.

I was so excited about the group prayers before the service and sensed that God was encouraging me to pray for our church more. We will grow in His love, in His power and in His Word, and each one of our members of this church will carry His love, His fragrance to our community and that we bring His light into the darkness. I really thanked God for using us for His wonderful purposes!

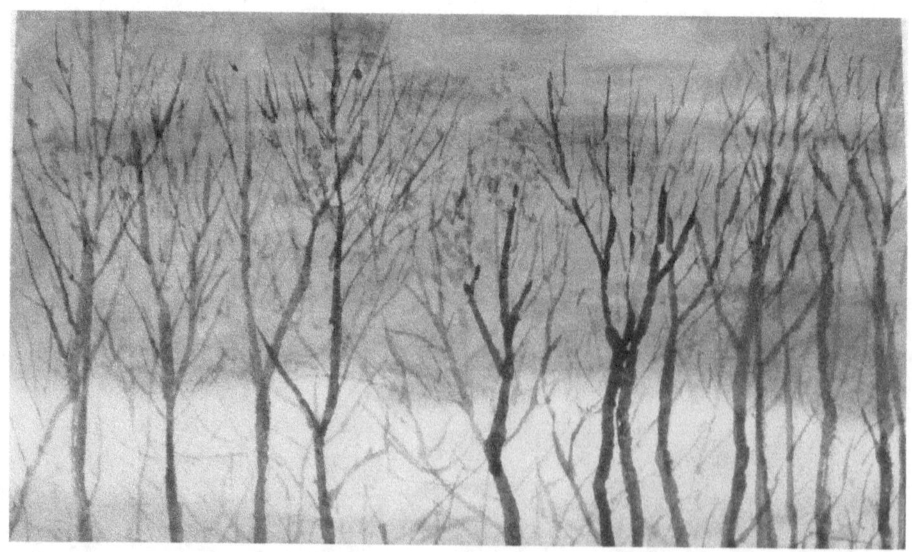

3
Time for Celebration

June 15, 2017

One day at the end of May, my friend, Sayomi called me from Japan and said, "I will be arriving at Mississauga on 6th of June, and I would like to stay there until 10th June. Is that okay with you?" I checked my calendar and said, "Yes, it's okay. I don't have many meetings in that week." Sayomi said she would fly from Japan to Buffalo and take a bus to Toronto and from Toronto to Mississauga. I told her that I would pick her up at Meadowvale GO Station.

I thought that Sayomi was coming at the right time. It is not cold, and it's not hot, and my garden is growing beautifully. When she arrives here, we may see some peonies opened. I was so excited to have Sayomi at my house.

Sayomi had a good job in California, but she quit it and went back to Japan to look after her aunt, Mitoko. Mitoko did not have any children and asked Sayomi to be her adopted daughter, and Sayomi agreed with her about 10 years ago. When Sayomi heard her aunt was in a hospital, she went back to Japan immediately.

Since then Sayomi called me often, at least once a week, sometimes twice or thrice a week. Every time she called me, I heard bad news, and I've worried about her, and also my heart ached. Sayomi told me that her parents' house was completely demolished by an earthquake and her aunt's house was half-demolished. Her parents were living with their relatives in their home and her aunt was still living in a damaged house. Sayomi had to find a place for her aunt, Mitoko, very quickly. This was bad enough news, but still she had more. For some reason, when Sayomi went back to Japan, Mitoko hated her so badly. She did not want to be with Sayomi, not only that, she told everybody, her neighbours, relatives, friends, her doctors and nurses, even Sayomi's parents how bad a person Sayomi is, and she made a big mistake making Sayomi her adopted child.

I listen to Sayomi's story, but I did not know how to respond to it. It was awful, nobody could take such rejection. I just said, "Sayomi ask God if it's his will to look after your aunt. If it is not His will, you better stop it, because you can't look after a person who hates you so much." Then Sayomi said, "I can't stop it, because I promised her."

Sayomi kept on calling me and told me so much bad news, and I was overwhelmed by that, but I did not know how to pray. I heard not only Mitoko, but her relatives disliked Sayomi and started saying bad things about her also. Sayomi was surrounded by strong enemies and they wanted to destroy a child of God. We have to line up with God.

One day, I said to God, "Lord, please forgive Sayomi's aunt, Mitoko, and Sayomi's relatives who hate her, and if Sayomi made any mistakes, please forgive her too." Since I prayed this prayer, I was able to pray for Sayomi, and I really thanked God. We have to line up with God and we have to go with His rules. We must be careful, I thought.

The next time Sayomi called me and reported more bad news. I said to her, "Sayomi, forgive your aunt, okay? If you can't forgive her, don't pray for her. It does not work." Then she said to me, "Okay, I will." I thanked God in my heart and asked them to strengthen Sayomi and bless her. I also told her, "Sayomi, you are surrounded by enemies. Be careful of everything you say. When you pray, don't ask for your desire, or your wish, but ask God's perfect will be done in this situation." Then she said, "Okay, I will." I was amazed by her answer. Even though she was hurt, she wanted to line up with God.

I also introduced her to Deric Prince's 'Blessing or Curse You Can Choose.' How to handle people who speak bad things against you. He wrote "Condemn the words spoken against you, but forgive and bless the person, then you will be blessed by God."

I told Sayomi, "No matter what people say against you, our heavenly Father does not see you like that. You are loved by God, and also precious in his eyes. So, condemn the bad words against you, but forgive the person and bless the person."

Sayomi said, "I will do that."

One day, I prayed for Sayomi at our Bible study. When I prayed for God's will be done in this situation, and asked His blessing over Sayomi, the ladies agreed, and Elli prayed for her.

Only a few days later, Sayomi called me and said, "Akemi, it is so amazing, everything has changed completely. My aunt Mitoko is in a hospice. She had a severe pain in her stomach and a doctor found a big cancer in her pancreas, and it is already at stage four. The doctor said he can't treat her anymore, but just gave her painkillers."

Sayomi said, "I don't have to look for a seniors' home for my aunt anymore. I just want her to have peace." I encouraged Sayomi to pray continually for God's will to be done.

Within two months, Mitoko passed away and Sayomi arranged a funeral and she was able to pay all the expenses.

Next time Sayomi called me she was cleaning out her aunt's house, and two storehouses. She had to empty a huge house and storehouses to ask the government to demolish them. It was a huge job and almost impossible, but she found Christian volunteers, and they helped her a lot. She reported to me that the first time seven people came to clean the house and the second time eleven people came with a huge truck and got rid of lots of things from the house.

God was so kind to Sayomi and blessed her in so many ways. She reported to me of so many wonderful things from Japan. I was so happy to hear that. We thanked God a lot on the phone.

On the 4th of May, Sayomi called me from Japan and said "I will be in Mississauga in two days. When I arrive in Toronto, I will call you."

"Alright, that's good. I will pick you up at the GO station. Have a wonderful trip."

"Yes, I will," she said, and continued, "by the way, I got a job."

"What? When?"

"Yesterday. I found an ad and applied. Yesterday I went for an interview. An 80-year-old lady owns a company she was looking for a successor. When she saw me, she said, "I like you. I want you to take over my company. I will teach you for the next five years and then I will retire. I will be a stockholder. You will run my company. She was so kind to me, and I got job."

I was stunned. God is pouring His blessings over her unlimitedly. I really thanked God for that.

On the sixth of June, at 10:30 I picked up Sayomi at the Meadowvale GO Station. We spent a very peaceful time in my house. We ate lunch in the garden looking at the beautiful flowers. We thanked God and praised him a lot.

Sayomi said, "I never forget to forgive and bless, and ask His will be done, not my desire."

"Yes, we will do that continually and we will see His endless blessings over."

It is so wonderful to live our lives with God.

4

Use My Paintings for Your Glory

July 23rd, 2017

This spring I could not take an art class at Visual Arts Mississauga. When I called the office and inquired about the spring course, a lady said that they did not have an advanced watercolour course this spring, because our teacher had a problem and could not teach. The lady assured me that they have a fall course, so I did not take an art class this spring. I really enjoyed our teacher Sherell Girard before, I just hoped everything was okay with her.

This spring, I stayed home and painted many cards. I got some quite large envelopes, 15 centimeters by 22 centimeters, and got water-color paper and painted many flowers on them. I painted yellow roses in a basket, pink roses in a vase, blue bachelor buttons, purple clematis, etc. I truly enjoyed painting cards whenever I had time. I also painted a bird's bath with four birds in it.

When my friends' birthdays approached, I sent my hand painted cards to them, and I was happy to do that. One time my friends Rita, Dianne, and I, visited our friend Inez and Waterloo Hospital. Inez was suffering from cancer in her bones. I took my hand-painted card of yellow roses in a basket, and asked Rita and Dianne to write something and sign it.

Inez was a very faithful and kind sister in the Lord. She took Rita and me to the Messiah concert a couple of times and we enjoyed the beautiful concerts.

When I gave Inez my hand-painted card, she was very pleased and put it on the windowsill. We prayed over her, and I really desired God's peace over her. We had a good visit, and we were pleased with what we did that day. Only in a couple of months, I heard that Inez was moved to a hospice. Cancer had spread all over her body, and they decided not to fight it anymore. Then only two days later, I got news that Inez had passed away. It was such shocking news, and I felt so sad. But I knew so well that Inez is with the Lord without pain and suffering anymore. What a triumphant homecoming! She had a very good life to come to know Jesus while she was on the earth. I thank God for that.

When Rita, Christine, and I attended Inez's funeral, I was so pleased for her victorious life. Yes, she went through many difficult times, but she always trusted God and she is with him in heaven now.

At the funeral home, we were invited to a special room where Inez's photos were displayed. I saw many of her favorite things on a little table, like her Bible, her devotional book, and I saw my hand-painted card there too. I was surprised to see it. When I talked with Inez's sister, she said to me, "Thank you, Akemi, for this beautiful card. Inez watched that card until she died."

I was so glad to hear that. If God can use even my painting to comfort His people, and give them peace and joy, I am so pleased. I thanked God in my heart, knowing that I don't have to do big things to please God, but just what I can do. He will use it, like a glass of water to my friends. I came home from Inez's funeral with great encouragement and thanked God for that.

Only a few days ago, I received a short letter from my friend Zeny in the Philippines. I met Zeny about 15 years ago. She and her husband visited their son's house on our street. Zeny's husband was a pastor, and they heard that I lost my husband and was suffering. Zeny kindly visited me and spent time with me. When Zeny prayed over me, I thought that I had to pray for her, and I prayed over her. Then she started crying. After she cried, she said, "Can I visit you again with my husband?"

"Yes, it's okay with me," I said.

A couple days later, Zeny and her husband visited me officially. I remember I baked an apple cake and made a cup of tea for them. We spent a good time together. They prayed over me and encouraged me.

Since then, Zeny sent me letters often and I sent her by hand-painted cards. Meanwhile, Zeny's husband passed away, and she went through a very hard time, but she never stopped sending me her letters. I sent my book Akemi's Journal to comfort her. I thanked God for a faithful friend He gave to me. Zeny and I both lost our husbands and suffered a lot, but we both are finding out the goodness of God in our lives. Because of our struggles and sufferings, God is making us more patient and stronger. I am so thankful for what God is doing in Zeny's life and in my life.

When I opened Zeny's letter, there was a piece of paper with a picture of a lighthouse, and on it was written "light of my life."

Zeny wrote:

Dear Akemi,

I truly thank God in all my remembrance of you (Philp 1:3), for you have been His blessing to me from the beginning. All hand-painted cards you have sent have been framed and occupy a wall in our house. They are a delight to see every day. Dear friend, thank God for your heart. May he put a hedge of protection around you and keep you safe.

Love, Zeny

What a beautiful letter I received. It was so good to know somebody is enjoying my paintings. I truly thanked God for that. If my paintings make anybody happy, I am so pleased and want to paint more. If God can use my paintings to comfort people or give them joy, I am so happy. I said to God, "Lord, thank you for giving me this life. I am yours. Use me in any way to bring glory to you, even through paintings, writing, gardening, anything and everything. Thank you, Father. You are a wonderful God and I'm happy to be yours!

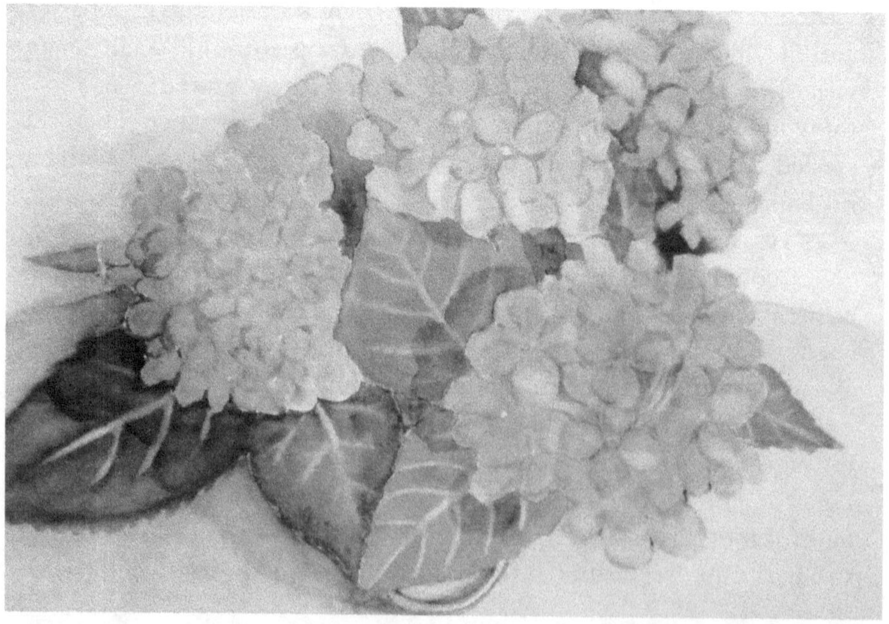

5

I had a Car Accident

October 11, 2017

On a beautiful Sunday morning on June18th, while I was driving to our church, I turned to the left a little too late, and was hit by an oncoming car. I moved my car to a nearby shopping plaza, but I knew I could not drive my car anymore. I talked to the man who hit my car. He had already called the police. I found out that he was coming home from church, and I was going to church. I called one of my trustees, Janis Flower, and asked her to come and be with me. She was going to see her father at Sunnybrook Hospital in Toronto, but she changed her mind and said that she would come soon.

While I was waiting for Janis, I said to God, "Father, I am sorry. I made a big mistake. Please forgive me." Then God said to me, "Have you forgiven yourself? Forgive yourself too." I said, "thank you." Janis came soon and was with me.

It took a long time, but a police officer came, and he talked to both of us and he gave me a ticket, and we had to call a tow truck. I removed everything from my car and put them into Janis' car, and my car was towed to a collision place. I said goodbye to the gentleman who hit my car and Janis and I came home.

Janice called my insurance broker and dealt with it efficiently. I was so thankful for that. She even called Gary and reported my accident. When I talked to him, he said, "Are you okay? Are you injured?" I said, "I am okay, but my car isn't."

"That's okay, we can deal with it." I asked him to help me when I went to buy a new car, and he agreed.

In spite of this disaster, things moved very quickly, and a rental car arrived soon, and I practiced driving the powerful rental car with Janis.

I was so thankful for her help all day.

Only three days later, Gary came after his work and drove me to a car dealer, Addison Chevrolet, and we found the smallest car. I did a test drive, and it was much easier than the rental car, so I obtained a car. On the 29th of June, a salesman came to pick me up and drove me to the dealer. After I paid the dealer, I drove home. It was very fast, and I thanked God for that.

In a few days, I asked Anita to come with me to pay the traffic ticket. I also had to go to the collision place to pick up by car keys and the license plate. Rita came with me and helped me. When I returned the rental car, Dianne helped me, and she drove me home afterwards. I really thanked God that I was able to do all these things with my good friends' help.

It was very hectic, but eventually everything settled down. I got used to driving a different car and drove to our church every Sunday, and I truly thanked God for that.

It was quite peaceful until August 10th, when I received a letter from the Ministry of Transportation, and found out that because of my car accident, I had to take an eye test, written test, and a road test within 60 days.

I took out a driving guidebook and started reading and memorizing the traffic signs and regulations. Then my friend Joe visited me and found out on his cell phone where to go and promised me to take me one day to the driving test place. I really thanked him.

On the 12th of August, Anita invited me for their cell group's barbeque, and sent her son to pick me up. At Anita's backyard, I talked to Anita's husband Feroze, about my driving test. He said, "I will teach you, Akemi. Don't worry. I taught my son Ben how to drive and he passed the test." I really thanked him.

On the 17th of August, Anita called me and invited me to her home to do the driving written test on the computer. I visited her home again and practiced the computer test the whole morning and then came home. Then soon Joe called me and said, "Akemi, have you visited the driving test place in Brampton?" I said "No, not yet." Then he said, "I would like to drive you there so that you know how to get there." I thanked him and we decided to visit the test place on that afternoon.

Soon Joe visited me. I put the letter from the Ministry of Transportation in my purse and we went there. When we arrived, there were more than 100 people lined up to register from the entrance of the building to the side of the building. Joe went to the inside of the building by himself and came back soon. I did not know what he did but he invited me into the building to register. Joe said, "Akemi, already we are here, let's try the written test today." I agreed, and waited quite a long time, but I was able to take the test on a computer and passed. I really thanked God for that and made an appointment for a road test on the 28th of September.

Feroze gave me driving lessons. He taught me so wonderfully and patiently. I had to drive on the highway and change the lanes to the left and the right. I was so scared and nervous about that, but I did it with Feroze's help. I even practiced parallel parking too. Feroze gave me altogether 20 lessons from August 18th to September 27th. We drove to the drive test place often and drove around there. He did everything he could, and I tried very hard, and I took the test on the 28th of September. I tried my best, but I was nervous about it, and I did not pass the test.

I was so discouraged! I made another appointment for the 2nd of November and my driver's license became a G1. I could not drive a car by myself. Somebody who has a driver's license had to be with me.

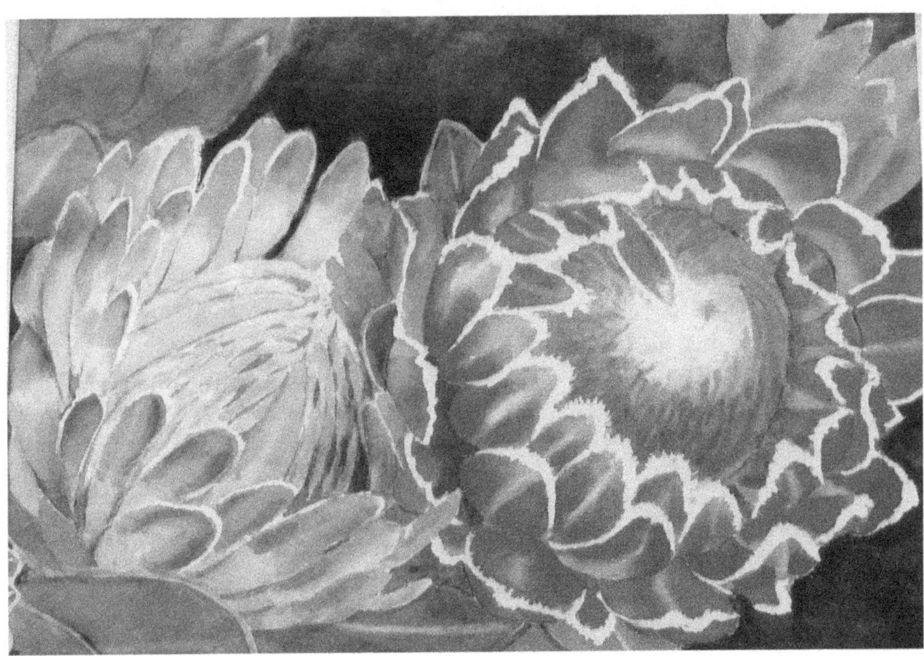

I did not know how to think or what to do. The only thing I could say was that I tried my best. The exam paper checked—too slow—in so many places. I felt so sorry for Feroze because he tried very hard to teach me.

He said, "Akemi, do not make any decision right now. You think about what to do next. Okay?"

I said, "Thank you."

Anita was with me when I drove home, and her son, Ben drove his car and came to my place, and Anita left with her son.

When I checked the exam paper, I realized that I can't fix my mistakes in a month, but I also knew it was very difficult to live my life without driving a car. I could not decide what to do for a few days, and I could not drive a car by myself anymore.

When I was struggling to decide what to do next, my sister, Sanae, called me from Japan and said that she had sent me a birthday gift. I thanked her and told her about my car accident and road test that I failed, and I said, "But I have one more opportunity to take a test in a month." Then she said, "Please don't take a second test. Listen to God and what he is saying to you. You tried your best and it did not work. God is telling you to stop driving a car. It's too dangerous for you. Call a taxi. If you have another accident, it's so dangerous for you and for other people. Please stop driving."

I just listened to my sister. She never talked to me like that before, and she never talked about God before. I just thanked her and finished our conversation on the phone.

Living without a car is very difficult, but I can't afford another accident. I had to put everything into God's hands, saying to myself, "God carried me through beautifully up to now, and he will carry me through from now on too." When I lost my husband, I did not believe that I would be able to survive, but God help me so wonderfully. Now, I really have to trust God more than before.

I sensed a peace from God starting to come into my heart and thanked God for showing me a new direction.

I said in my prayer, "Father, thank you for the last 17 years. I was able to drive a car. Now a new chapter will start in my life. I will live my life without driving a car. I just thank you that you will help me again. I am so glad that I am your daughter. Thank you."

6

I Started a New Chapter

October 27, 2017

A big change came to my life after I failed the driving test on the 28th of September. I needed lots of adjustment and lots of planning, but I thought what I truly needed was wisdom from God. Without panicking and disappointment, I had to move on one step at a time, trusting God, my heavenly Father, who knows everything that is happening in my life. He is bigger than any problem I face on the earth.

It was very unfortunate, but the only consolation was that I tried my best. No matter what, I had to move on. I decided to visit Shirley and Tracy, mother and daughter, who live in the house across the street from mine. Shirley doesn't drive a car, only Tracy drives. They are very kind neighbours and have helped me a lot in the past.

One evening, I visited them. I said to Shirley, "Shirley, I would like to ask you a very important question."

"Yes, what is it, Akemi?"

"I failed the driving test, and I can't drive a car anymore. When you go to do grocery shopping, would you take me with you?"

Shirley thought awhile and said, "Akemi, it's not convenient for you, because we take so long to do our grocery shopping. We go to two or three stores and take a long time, but Tracy will take you some other day. You and Tracy can do grocery shopping after she comes home from her work."

I really thanked her. Then Shirley added, "If you need one or two items immediately, just call me and I will call my daughter and she will pick it up for you on her way home." What a kind answer I received! I really thanked them. I also asked Shirley about bus tickets for seniors and I learned that I could obtain senior bus tickets at Shoppers Drug Mart. I decided to buy them.

A few days later, I asked my neighbour's grandfather, Tim, to sit with me in my car so that I would be able to do shopping, and he agreed. I went to Shoppers Drug Mart with Tim and obtained 10 senior bus tickets. Tim suggested I should do my grocery shopping too, so I went to Metro and did some grocery shopping.

That was the last time I drove my car. The next time I had an appointment at physio, I took a bus. I had to wait about 7 minutes, and had to wear thick socks, because it was quite a cold morning, but when a bus arrived at the entrance of our street, I was the only passenger, and it was very comfortable. It took exactly 10 minutes to arrive at Meadowvale Town Centre. After I finished my treatment at physio, I did some shopping and came home by bus.

By car was in the garage, but I started sensing peace in my heart and knew that I could adjust to the new life easier than I thought, and I really thanked God for that.

My good friends, Jeffrey and Suzanne Chung started taking me to our church, and drove me home. I felt so comfortable and thanked them. On our way home they went to a grocery store on two occasions and I did grocery shopping too.

Our home group leader, Elli, called me often and offered to take me grocery shopping. She drove to a naturopathic doctor one day and on the way home I did grocery shopping. I was so thankful for that.

My friend Debbie asked me to paint her daughter and her fiancé's picture. They were holding hands in clear water with a small waterfall as background with many trees. Debbie said that they became engaged in that water, and this painting would be her wedding gift for them. I painted it with joy, and I had a good time painting it. When I finished painting it, I called Debbie and told her to pick up the painting and also asked her that when she goes to the art store to frame the painting to take me with her, and she agreed.

One day Debbie came, and we went to De Serres to frame the painting. While she was ordering the frame, I did some shopping at the store. Then she took me to Fabric Land and Staples, and I did lots of shopping. While we were in her car, Debbie asked me, "How much do I owe you for that painting?"

I said, "Debbie, I don't need money. When I have to go out, would you take me out?"

"Of course, I will."

"That's good." I was so thankful for that too.

On the 19th to 21st of October, our church had a conference with Keir and Callie Taylor from Africa. On the Friday night after Keir's teaching, I talked to Pastor James Colgan. He asked me, "How are you doing, Akemi?"

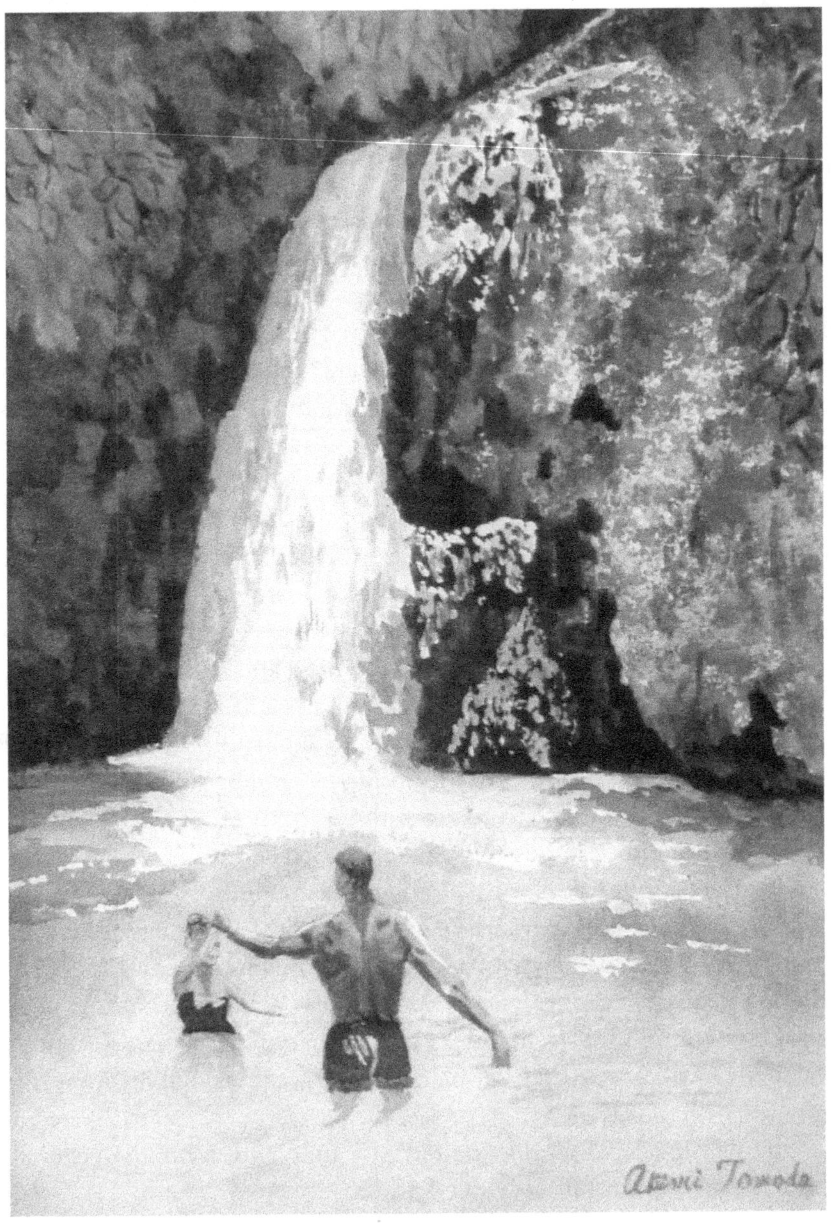

I told him about what happened in my life. I did not pass a road test, and now I have to live without driving a car. He was really concerned about me. I said, "But Pastor James, I started driving a car when I was age 63, right after my husband's death. I was so nervous driving a car. If I have another car accident and injure myself or other people, it's worse. I can't take it."

Then he said, "If you have peace, that's a good thing. Let me know when you need help for grocery shopping or anything. We will arrange people to help you." I was so moved by his kindness and said, "Thank you so much. I feel so safe," and shook his hand. Then he gave me a big hug, and immediately I fell on the floor. The Holy Spirit joined us. It was really something!

One day Anita called me and asked me if I needed any shopping. I said yes and told her that I wanted to go to Sears and also wanted to buy a buggy. Soon Anita and her mother came, and we went out shopping together. Anita drove me to Walmart, but all the buggies were sold out, so we went to Sears. After Sears, she took me too Longo's, and I did grocery shopping too. I was very thankful for her kind help. When Anita was driving home, she said, "I will take you to some other store to buy a buggy next time." I really thanked her.

Our home group leader, Elli, often checking to see if I needed something. On the 20th of October, we had our home group and started studying the book of Revelations. Elli prepared it so well. Right after we finished studying, Elli said, "Akemi, let's go grocery shopping. I will take you," and she drove me to Longo's and I did grocery shopping there. I was so thankful for her kindness. I thanked God for His kind help by surrounding me with many wonderful friends to meet all my needs. I am so blessed that I am a part of His family. Every day when I go to bed, I thank God from the bottom of my heart.

Almost one month has passed since I decided not to drive a car. I feel so strange, but I don't miss driving a car at all. It was so handy, but I was so nervous every time I drove a car, and I am totally free from that. Yes, it is inconvenient. I have to check the bus schedule, or I have to call a taxi, but I am free from nervousness and I have started sensing the peace of God in my life. I am so thankful for that! Recently I changed my dentist to a closer place where I can walk in less than five minutes.

Let us see how it works one day at a time with a big thanksgiving towards our wonderful Heavenly Father.

7

He will Meet all My Needs

November 11th, 2017

When I decided not to drive a car anymore, I had to do something about my car, but I knew so well that I could not handle it by myself. When Gary came, I asked him about selling my car, and he said, "I am not good at selling cars, Akemi. I have two motorcycles and I want to sell one, but it's very difficult."

I thought I had to ask somebody else and so mentioned it to Janis. Then she said that she knows a car mechanic, so she could ask him. I thanked her.

One night when I was lying on my bed, a thought came to my mind so clearly that I should contact my salesman, who sold me my car at Addison Chevrolet. I remembered when I bought that car from Bob, he was so kind to me. That time Gary helped me so much.

When he came back from the test drive and parked the car at the parking lot of the dealer, Bob asked us, "May I ask what kind of relationship you have?"

Gary said immediately, "We are just friends."

I added, "I lost my husband 17 years ago, and I don't have any children. Gary has helped me since then, and he is my trustee now."

Then Bob said, "It's so beautiful. I would like to be one of your friends. Please think about me as one of your friends."

I said, "Thank you."

I thought that I must pray about it. The next day Rita visited me. While she was in the living room, I took out a letter from Bob, and said, "Rita this letter is from my car salesman Bob. I want to pray that God will give me favour to sell my car back to him." We prayed for God's favour on selling my car and asked that Bob would take my car back. When we finished our prayer, I asked Rita, "Shall I call him now?" Rita said, "I think we'd better visit him and talk to him face to face."

"Okay, that's good. Could you take me there one day?"

"Of course, I will," she replied.

A few days later when I talked to Rita on the phone, I asked her to take me to Addison Chevrolet when she was free, and she said, "Let's go this afternoon."

She came around 2 o'clock, and we went to the Addison dealership. When we arrived at the parking lot, and parked the car, Bob came out from the office and looked at us and said, "Oh Mrs. Tomoda, it's wonderful to see you. How are you?" I greeted him and introduced Rita and we were invited over to Bob's desk.

I mentioned what had happened when I did my driving test, and that I can't drive a car anymore and that I wanted to return my car back to the dealership. Then he said, "I am really sorry, but about your car I have to ask the manager. Can you wait here? I will go and ask him right now." He went to talk to the manager. Soon he came back and said, "Yes, we can take your car back, but the price is not the same."

"Of course, I know that," I said. He showed me quite a low price, but I was so glad that I did not have to sell my car by myself. They will do all the paperwork, and they did not have to do a test drive. I was so relieved. But I said, "I would like to talk to Gary, and I will let you know what to do." Then Bob said, "Just a minute. I will talk to the manager again." And he went to see the manager and when he came back, he offered me $500 more for my car.

"When you talk to Gary, please call me on my cell phone," he asked.

"Yes, I will. Thank you so much."

Rita drove me home. After Rita left, I soon called Gary, and told him about selling my car and he said, "The price is very low, but Akemi if you are okay, I think it is good."

"Okay, then I will go ahead."

"Okay."

I called Bob and told him that I accept his offer. Then he said, "I will pick up your car in two days."

But he called me the next day and asked me if I was at home that afternoon and he came with a young man with a screwdriver, and removed the license plates and gave me a cheque and asked me to sign the paper. I just signed the paper. That's all I did for selling my car. That was so easy. I truly thanked God for that.

The following day, I called my insurance broker and mentioned that I won't be driving a car anymore, and the lady promised to take care of the matter. I also called CAA and told them my intention. The lady said that she renewed my membership a few days ago, but she would cancel it immediately. It went so well. Only two days later, Rita took me to the Ontario license place, and returned the license plates, and the lady gave me a paper, and said she would send me money in a month. Everything went so well in a week. I felt so good about it and thanked God for that.

I lost my hair stylist last September. I have been going to the First Choice at Erin Mills Parkway and Millcreek for the last 16 years. A hair stylist, Widad Samaan, treated my hair nicely. She is a good hairstylist, and on top of that I found that she is a faithful Christian, and her grandfather was a pastor in Israel. I was so happy to go there. However, last September the salon was closed.

The last time I was there, Widad told me that she decided to work out of her house and gave me a card and invited me to go to her house for the next time. I said, "Yes, I will visit your house. Thank you."

Since I don't drive a car anymore, I can't do that. I have to go to the closest hairdresser. I asked my friends and found out that the closest hairdresser is at Meadowvale Town Centre. So, I decided to visit there the next time.

One night when I was in my bed, a thought came to me so strong that I should contact Widad. I thought that was very strange, but the next morning I called Widad, and talked to her. When I mentioned that I can't drive a car anymore that I can't visit her house, Widad said, "I am sorry, Akemi, but if you come to Erin Mills Town Centre in a taxi, I will go there and pick you up, and send you back there."

I said, "if you can come to Erin Mills Town Centre, you can come to my house. My house is not far from the Town Centre." Then Widad said, "Okay, I can do that. When you want to come, call me, we can decide on a day."

"Thank you so much. That would be so nice."

I was so happy and thanked God for that. I felt such relief and thanked God who surrounded me with such very kind people who helped me so wonderfully.

A couple of weeks later, I contacted Widad, and decided to do my hair on the 31st of October. When I said, "Shall I call you one day before to confirm?"

Then Widad said, "No, I will call you on the 30th." I really thanked her. In the evening of the 30th, Widad called me and told me that she would leave her house around 10 the following morning. The next morning when she arrived at my driveway, she called me, and we went to her house. Widad's house is so beautiful, and she invited me to her basement. There was a beautiful hair salon, and even soft music was playing. I felt so comfortable at her salon. She treated my hair as usual, and I felt so comfortable. She even offered me a cup of tea and a sweet during the treatment.

I was so blessed and thanked God for the wonderful gift! When she finished my hair, Widad showed me her house. Her house is so clean and well-organized. After she drove me home, I invited her to my art gallery and showed her my husband's and my artwork in my home.

I had a wonderful day, and my hair was nicely coloured and cut. I was so pleased.

When I decided not to drive a car anymore, I thought I would face many problems, but things are going so well, I truly thanked God for his wonderful help. He has surrounded me with very kind and warm-hearted people, and I have received wonderful help from many people.

"My God meets all your needs according to His glorious riches in Christ Jesus." ~ Philippians 4:20

I am experiencing God's faithfulness in my life. I am really thankful for that, and I have hope for my future because God is helping me. He is with me and He is in me.

8

Lord You are Awesome

November 21, 2017

About seven or eight years ago, my friend Gary introduced me to his co-worker Debbie, and asked me to alter her clothes. Debbie brought many pants to be shortened and dresses to be altered, and I fixed them. When she asked me the price of alteration, I said, "Debbie, these are free, because Gary does my yard work for free. I can't charge you." Debbie thanked me.

That was the beginning of our encounters. I learned little by little about Debbie every time she visited me with her clothes. She is from Guyana and her parents went to Guyana from China, and she has one son and two daughters. Eventually I met her son and daughters and altered their clothes too. About this time, I also found out that they believed in Buddhism. I did not say anything about their belief, but sometime later, I gave my book Akemi's Journals to Debbie and said, "I wrote lots about Gary in this book."

Debbie found out that I do watercolor paintings and started asking me to paint from her photos. She brought pictures of her brother's dog, her hydrangea, and I painted them. One time she brought a beautiful print of her son and his fiancé standing holding each other looking at the beautiful sunset beside the river. Debbie said, "It's going to be my wedding gift for them." I still remember it as I painted this picture very carefully, and when I finished painting it, I was so pleased. Debbie framed it and she thanked me. I started feeling very comfortable talking to Debbie and enjoyed meeting with her.

One year, she wanted to buy my book, and she said, "I would like to give your book to my sister, who lives in England, and she is a Christian. My brother and I are going to visit her. I would like to give her your book as a gift." So, I sold one book to her.

Debbie became a very good friend of mine and she was very kind to me too. In the year 2014, when my stereo set did not work at all, Debbie brought her brother over and he fixed it for me very quickly. Last year, my stereo set stopped working again. My husband bought this stereo set when he quit smoking, so it is already a 20-year-old stereo. I thought that was it, and it was time to buy a new one.

Then Debbie found out about this problem and visited me with her brother again. This time he had to take my stereo home, but in a few months, he fixed it and brought it to my house. I was so blessed by their kindness. Every time I listen to classical music from the stereo, I remember Debbie and her brother's kindness.

Last fall, Debbie brought a print and asked me to paint them. One was her daughter and her fiancé standing in the water holding their hands, and a beautiful waterfall was surrounded by green leaves in the background. Debbie said that they became engaged in that river and that they are going to marry on the 11th of November. She also told me that this painting would be her wedding gift to her daughter. Another print was her sister's cat wearing a US flag on its neck. I agreed to paint them before their wedding, but I could not paint until the end of September because I was taking driving lessons from Anita's husband Feroze, so I painted them after my driving test.

I really enjoyed painting the two pictures of Debbie. In two days, I finished the two paintings and called her, and told her that her paintings were ready. I asked her to take me to De Serres when she would go to the store for the frame, so that I would do shopping there, and I told her that I did not pass my driving test. Debbie agreed to take me to the art store. In the morning of October, the 17th, Debbie came to pick me up, and we went to De Serres and while Debbie was ordering the frame for the painting, I was able to do some shopping. After De Serres, Debbie took me to Fabric Land and I did a little shopping there, and she took me to Staples where I bought paper pads and notebooks. I was so thankful for that. While she was driving, she asked me, "Akemi, how much do I owe you for that painting?" I said, "Debbie, I don't need money. When I need a ride could you give me one?"

"Of course, I will, that's good. Call me whenever you need a ride, okay?"

"Yes, I will. Thank you so much." I had a very nice time with Debbie and did lots of shopping. I was so thankful for that. On that day Debbie bought five pairs of pants and one jacket and one dress to be altered, and I altered them in a few days. I called Debbie and told her that her clothes were ready and asked her to take me to De Serres when she goes there next time, and she agreed.

On the 26th of October, Debbie took me to De Serres again and I did more shopping, and we went to Fabricland, and she even took me grocery shopping. When we came home, I invited her for a cup of tea, and we had a cup of tea in my living room. When we were talking, suddenly Debbie said, "I am praying to God every night."

"Which God?" I asked, because I knew she believed in Buddhism.

Then Debbie said, "The Lord. I start my prayer with the Lord's prayer."

"You mean 'Father, who art in heaven, hallowed be thy name' that one?" I asked.

"Yes that's the prayer," and she mentioned that she went to a Christian high school in Guyana, but she could not remember the Lord's prayer so she found it through the Internet, and is praying it every night. I was surprised and also so happy to hear that. I said, "That's wonderful! I'm so happy for you. Let me pray over you and bless you." I prayed over her and blessed her life with Jesus, and asked for a good job, because she lost her job and was looking for a new job.

After she left, I was in awe, and so excited about Debbie. I never mentioned about Jesus to her, what I did for her was fixing her clothes and painting her prints. I said to God, "Lord, how did you do that? You are amazing!"

I was so happy to find out that God can use anything and everything for his purpose, like sewing, painting, and writing. I said to God that night, "Lord, I am so happy to hear that Debbie is praying to you. I'm so glad to know that. Lord, use me for your glory. Use everything I do for your glory."

In a week, Debbie called me and asked me if I needed a ride. I said I did not need a ride then. Then she said, "Akemi, when you need a ride let me know, okay? And I would like to thank you for your prayer. I just got a job, thank you."

"That's wonderful. I'm so happy for you," I said, and said to the Lord in my heart, "Lord you are so good. Thank you, thank you, thank you!"

9

Closing 2017 with Big Hope

December 26, 2017

While I was reading the Bible in the morning of the 15th of December, Romans 15:13 came to my mind so strongly as if God was speaking to me. I read it repeatedly a few times.

May the God of hope fill you with all joy and peace as you trust in Him, so that you may overflow with hope by the power of the Holy Spirit. Romans 15:13

While I was meditating on the "hope" in this verse, another Bible verse came to my mind so clearly.

"I pray also that the eyes of your heart may be enlightened in order that you may know the "hope" to which He has called you the riches of his glorious inheritance in the Saints, and his incomparably great power for us who believe." Ephesians 1:18-19

I really thanked God for giving us hope. We can live our lives with overflowing hope, because He is with us. I sensed that the new chapter started in my life, and I can face the new year 2018 with a big hope.

Sitting in the living room, I looked at the snow-covered backyard. The Lord's Garden was cleaned neatly and resting under the white snow. It was so calm and peaceful. The year 2017 came to an end.

I faced many things this year, many difficulties and also many blessings. The difficulties were that I lost my driving license, and my nervous system was too sensitive. I had a car accident in June and had to take a driving test and failed. I thought it was very difficult to live my life without driving a car. It was a big change, but I was able to take a bus and a taxi, and my friends helped me so much, so it wasn't as bad as I thought. My shoulders and neck were getting lighter and I felt so relaxed without driving a car. I really thanked God for that.

My nervous system was too sensitive, and I experienced tingling in my legs for the last four years. So many friends prayed for me, and my family doctor checked my brain, neck, and spine with an MRI, but could not find the reason. I even visited a naturopathic health clinic. She helped me a lot, but the tingling came back badly. Also, I could not eat so many things because they affected my nervous system. But I was able to do everything I had to do. I really thanked God for that.

These were bad things, but I had so many good things too. I was able to look after the Lord's Garden again this year. I enjoyed being there. The flowers bloomed so beautifully, and every time I watered, the double rainbows appeared in the air. I talked and listened to God a lot in the garden this year too. I'm very thankful for that.

I had a special blessing on October the 14th. Seven of my close friends got together and celebrated my birthday at my home. They brought the food that I could eat, and celebrated my 80th birthday with delicious food and lots of prayers. Everyone prayed over me and blessed my future with the Lord. That was so special! I felt that God joined the celebration, and I received such encouragement from that. I really thanked my precious friends, Rita Gervais, Janis Orr, Heather Caswell, Elli Murack, Dianne Schleifer, Carol Hay and Janis Flowers.

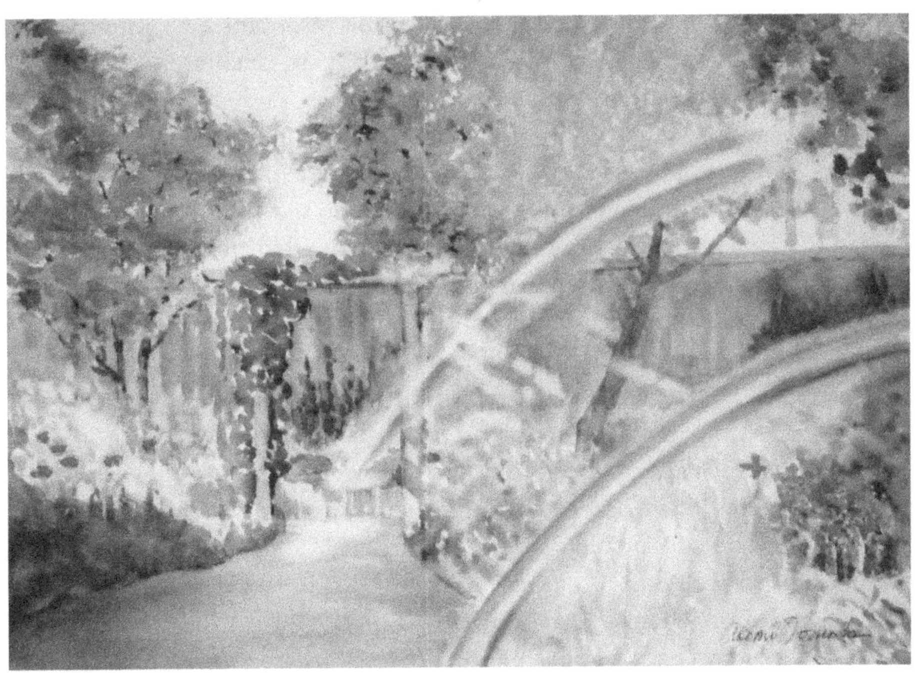

In November I had a special blessing. I visited my family doctor on the 6th of November. I prayed for my visit to Dr. Sarangiwala the night before and asked God for his blessing over my visit to the doctor. I also prayed while I was waiting for the doctor in the small examination room. I prayed God's blessing over me. When the doctor came, she renewed my prescriptions. I did not talk about my tingling legs for many years, because I knew that she could not do anything about it, but this time I mentioned it and asked, "I wonder if I can take Lyrica for my nervous system. Can I try it?" Then she said, "What?" I mentioned that I saw on TV and found out that Lyrica helps painful nervous systems. Then she said, "Oh Lyrica. I can prescribe that. I will give you the weakest one 50 mg. Let's try it for one month and then come back and see me."

I went to the pharmacy and got Lyrica. That night when I went to bed, I took one pill with a prayer to avoid any side effects and also to help my nervous system to calm down. When I woke up the next morning, I did not have the tingling anymore. I was so happy that I thanked God a lot, and I cried. It was so wonderful. After four years, I am tingling free. Thank you, Father! It was so good, I am now taking a pill every night with much thanksgiving towards God.

In December, I received a big surprise from my publisher, Cheryl Antao-Xavier. She invited me for the book celebration at Kingsman Centre on the 3rd of December. She was going to celebrate six authors and their new books and invited me to come around 4:00 o'clock.

This spring, I was wondering about publishing my second book or not. I had enough essays to do that. Then suddenly Cheryl called me, so I asked her to visit me sometime. She visited me soon and we talked, and I decided to publish my second book. Cheryl visited me often and one time she took the album of my watercolor paintings and a sketchbook. I received my new books at the end of the summer, and I was so pleased because Cheryl put so many of my watercolor paintings and sketches in the books. I was so happy, I thought they were such a good way to celebrate my 80 years of life.

Cheryl mentioned about the book celebration, but she never mentioned to me that I had to speak in that gathering. When she visited me a week before the day, we celebrated our books, I asked about my speech, and she said, "Yes please. I want you to speak about your book and ask your friends to read from your book."

I had to prepare a speech and asked my friends to read from my book. I asked Janis Flowers and Elli Murack, and they said okay.

I prepared my speech, but when I was preparing my speech, I realized that my books were published by God's help. I met a wonderful English teacher Eleanor Sproule, and she told me to present one essay every time she came, and I decided to write about the goodness of God in my life. I enjoyed writing God's goodness in my life so much that I kept on writing for 14 years, until my teacher went to Heaven. After Eleanore, her husband Keith checks my essays. God provided wonderful teachers in my life. I also met a creative writing teacher Anthazia Kader at the Older Adult Centre and she read my essays and suggested that I should publish my book. She introduced me to Cheryl, and she published my first book. I did not plan anything, God sent me people at the right time and my books were published. I really thanked God for that.

At the book celebration my five friends came to celebrate with me. All together 50 to 60 people with six authors got together. When I spoke, I emphasized God's great help and His kindness in my life. I also mentioned the importance of thanksgiving. Janis read a part of my book, and Elli read another part of my book. We all enjoyed visiting with good snacks and drinks, and new books. Two hours passed quickly, and Janis drove me home. I really thanked God for that day.

So, the year 2017 wasn't bad at all. I received so many blessings from God and also was given an encouraging Bible verse.

May the God of hope fill you with all joy and peace as you trust in Him so that you may overflow with hope by the power of the Holy Spirit.

I look forward to the year 2018 with big hopes in my heart.

10

The Year 2018 Started

January 15, 2018

The year 2018 started very peacefully, even though the weather was so severe with very cold temperatures and lots of snow. I felt such peace starting the new year, and I thanked God for that.

A very strange thing happened this year, which was that I started cleaning my house like I had never done before. I started cleaning the kitchen, cleaning the walls and the cabinets and the floor so neatly with Fantastic, and cleaned the oven inside and out, and even painted the kitchen cabinets here and there. I could not believe what I was doing, but I could not stop it. When I finished the kitchen, I went to the basement, and I cleaned, painted and even chiseled to remove 40 years of dust and stains. Then I cleaned the upstairs so neatly. My house became so clean and comfortable like 40 years ago. I was so pleased, but I often wondered why I was cleaning the house so seriously and also why I was so content to do the cleaning job. While I was cleaning the basement, a thought came to me as if I was cleaning the house of God and this satisfied me tremendously. Then the Bible verse came to my mind:

"Don't you know that you yourselves are God's temple and that God's spirit lives in you?" 1 Corinthians 3:16

And suddenly I had a huge desire to clean the temple of God spotless so that the Holy Spirit can live happily and comfortably.

I was so thankful about what God taught me through the cleaning of my house. This is my purpose for this year to clean the temple of God, removing all junk and dust in my life, removing my own desires and plans and even my own goals for my life, and let the Holy Spirit move freely in my life as he desires. I was so pleased and thanked God for the way I started this year.

The first Sunday of this year, on the 7th of January, my good friends Jeffrey and Suzanne Chung gave me a ride to our church, Life House church in Streetsville. Pastor James Colgan quoted from Isaiah 55:8-9

"For my thoughts are not your thoughts neither are your ways my ways, declares the Lord. As the heavens are higher than the earth so are my ways higher than your ways and my thoughts than your thoughts."

And he said, "We must seek His ways not our own, His plans not our own."

I was so pleased to hear that, I said, "Yes!" in my heart. I really thanked God for the right direction we were choosing. The year 2018 started very hopefully.

On the 9th of January, my good friend Anita, came to a small home group. This time Anita called me before she left her house and told me that she would take me out for grocery shopping first, and then we could spend time with the Lord. I really thanked her for her kindness. She took me to Longo's and Freshco and I was able to do lots of shopping. I am very thankful for my many kind friends that God sends me.

After our shopping, we spent precious time in my clean living room. We thanked God as usual, and asked God for His will to be done in our lives and our families' lives. His best will be done. His plans and His purpose for our lives will be fulfilled. We also talked about God's discipline. He disciplines us for our good so that we can share in His Holiness.

We spent a beautiful time with lots of thanksgivings and praises. I was so blessed to have such a precious time in my house.

The cleaning of my house did not stop. I continuously cleaned here and there all over my house. It is so strange because I did not see many dirty spots before, but this year I saw many dirty spots on the walls and doors, all over my house. I kept on cleaning with joy in my heart, and every time I cleaned, I thanked God for this clean house.

On the 11th of January, Rita called me and invited me to go grocery shopping. I had enough groceries but went out with her and enjoyed spending time together, and also I bought so many groceries. It was fun, and I enjoyed it very much. When Rita drove me home, I thanked her and said, "I would like to start this year with prayers with you. When you have time could you come and pray with me?" Then she said, "I will come tonight. Let's do it."

That evening Rita came, and we prayed together with lots of thanksgiving and praises. It was so wonderful to invite God's will and His direction into all our ways. I was so blessed to start this year with prayer. I had a good time with Rita and thanked God for that.

In the afternoon of the 17th of January, our Bible study started at my house. Elli, Dianne and Rita came, and we had a beautiful meeting. As usual we worshiped God with soft worship music and praised God, and we had communion, and studied the Bible in Revelations. Elli prepared so neatly, and we had a blessed time together. We started this year with a wonderful meeting. This is a precious gift from God and I truly thanked God for that.

In that meeting while I was meditating quietly, a memory came back to me so clearly. While Sayomi stayed with me for a week last November, Rita took Sayomi and me to CTF Toronto for a prophetic meeting, and we all were prophesied over. I was prophesied over by a lady called Penny. She said, "Akemi, you are holding Jesus' hand and walking together towards God's heart. You are walking step by step with Jesus towards going deeper and deeper into God's heart. Some people run to Him, and some people jump into Him, but you are walking. I bless your journey with Jesus."

I remember this prophecy so clearly and I thought this is my destiny for my life. I will walk with Jesus one step at a time with thanksgiving towards God's heart. What a blessed journey and I thanked God for the wonderful way I started in the year of 2018!

11

The Month of Sewing

February 28, 2018

This winter we had lots of snow in December and January. Snow fell and fell on my front and backyard and they were covered with thick snow. The temperature was much colder than the last few years. I cleaned the driveway many times, and I was busy.

I also enjoyed looking at the snow-covered backyard. It was so peaceful. All the perennials were sleeping under the snow. This is the time of rest for the plants.

In February, we had several mild days, and we did not have snow for many days. Occasionally it rained. I did not have to clear the driveway. I had lots of free time and decided to do some sewing. The end of the last year my friend, Ingrid, sent me a big box of fabric from Germany as a gift. When I opened the box, there were six different kinds of fabric in it. They were so classy and such beautiful, good material. I was in awe, because I could not find this kind of good quality of fabric here. Last year, I visited a fabric store many times, but came out without buying anything.

I decided to make a jacket from beautifully woven black and red material. It required lots of patience, but I enjoyed sewing a jacket with thanking God for a wonderful friend He has given me.

The first time I met Ingrid was in 1970. When I came to Canada, Ingrid and her husband, Yasu, invited my husband Ken and me for dinner at their apartment. Ingrid was the first person who invited me for dinner in this country. We had a good time. Yasu and Ingrid invited us often and we invited them for dinner two.

One of those days after dinner, while we were talking, Ingrid started talking about Christianity. She said, "Christians are believing God blindly." At that time, I could not speak English, but I thought that I had to say something, and said, "But I am a Christian, and I love Jesus." There was an awkward quietness for a long time, and Yasu said, "That is why I don't want to talk about religion." It is already 48 years ago, but I still remember that night so clearly.

Yasu and Ingrid were our good friends in Canada, and we spent many times visiting conservation parks and enjoyed delicious lunches and friendship together, but we never talked about Christianity again.

While I was sewing my jacket, all these memories came back to me. I lined my jacket and put on the collar and sleeves. I made buttonholes and put on buttons. I enjoyed every step and thanked God that I am still able to sew my own clothes.

The weather was still mild, and we had rain instead of snow. When I finished my jacket, I decided to make a pantsuit from some gray, beautiful wool and started cutting the fabric. I thought how Ingrid has good taste and she is so generous. I am so blessed to have such a kind friend! While I was catching the gray wool, my thoughts went back to many years ago.

Yasu and Ingrid bought a nice house in Oakville, and we bought a townhouse in Mississauga. We got together often and enjoyed our friendship. Soon Ingrid moved back to Germany, and some time later Yasu followed her. Since then, I did not hear anything from them for many years. After a few years, Yasu came back to Canada, and I learned that they had divorced, and Ingrid had married a German man.

I truly thought that our friendship had ended, but Ingrid contacted us again, and one day she visited us with her new husband. We had a nice time together. Since then, Ingrid is back in my life. She calls me on my birthday every year and sings 'Happy birthday to you' to me and celebrates my birthday. I also call on her birthday and sing 'Happy birthday to you.'

After a few years, Ingrid lost her husband, and I lost my husband. She lost her mother too. We both went through a very hard time. When I lost my husband, Ingrid visited me and comforted me. She gave me a teddy bear, and I still keep it.

A few years ago, when Ingrid called me, we talked a lot. She started talking about Jesus. I was shocked to hear that, but I was also so happy at the same time. Suddenly she talked about what she was doing to help two Native families in North Dakota in the USA by sending clothes and other goods regularly. She said, "I don't have any children. I don't have to keep my money for them. I would like to help people. She also said, "Akemi, God bless you!" I was so happy to hear from her, I also said, "God bless you, Ingrid."

I don't know when she became a believer of Jesus. I don't know what God did to her, suddenly I have a wonderful Christian friend in Germany. I truly thank God for that.

The last time Ingrid called me on my birthday, I told her that I wasn't driving a car anymore. Then she said, "Akemi, I think that is good for you. You are free from stress. Now you have lots of time. I will send you some material so that you can sew.

I enjoyed sewing in the month of February, and made one jacket, one pant suit, and two tops. I truly enjoyed sewing and also enjoyed remembering my relationship with Ingrid.

God prepared a wonderful friend in Canada when I moved to Canada. And she is still a precious friend of mine. She is not only a friend, but she is a precious sister in the Lord now. I thank God for the marvelous work for Ingrid.

In the last two weeks, we had unusually mild weather and lots of rain. The snow melted completely, and green grass has appeared.

A new spring is coming soon. I really thanked God for the way I spent this winter.

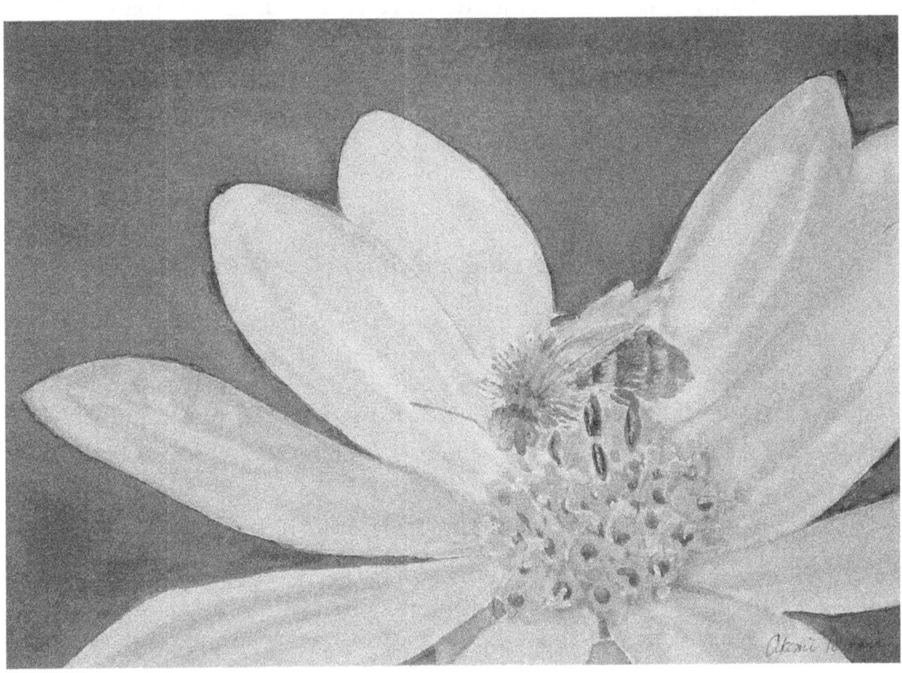

12

The New Season Started

March 21st, 2018

On the morning of March 20th, I was sitting on the sofa in my living room and watching the backyard. Snow had melted completely, and the green grass had appeared. When I looked at the flower garden, I saw new shoots here and there. There were short green leaves of tulips and daffodils and red leaves of hostas and spiderworts and many other shoots all over the garden. The new spring had started, and winter was gone. Even though the temperature was still cold, the plants were showing the sign of a new spring. This is the season! I thanked God. "Lord, thank you, a new season is coming in your garden. I will enjoy your beautiful garden this year again. I also thank you for a new season and a new chapter in my life. You have taught me and changed me. I'm so thankful for that."

The last five years, the Lord taught me so much. I went through a very tough time. It started with Acts 9:16. When I was reading the Bible Acts 9:16 hit me.

It says:

9:15 "But the Lord said, Anania, go! This man is my chosen instrument to carry my name before the Gentiles and their King and before the people of Israel."

9:16 "I will show him how much he must suffer for my name."

I wondered if it was only Paul or for us too. I wanted to know so badly, so I asked God about this. Then he said to me, "I loved Paul as much as I loved my son Jesus."

Then later while I was reading the Bible, God gave me Romans 5:7. It hit me so strongly.

"Not only so, but we also rejoice in our sufferings, because we know that suffering produces perseverance, perseverance character, and character hope. Romans 5:3-4.

It really bothered me, because I felt that I don't want to go through suffering anymore. I thought that I suffered enough in my life when I lost my husband.

Then soon the Lord challenged me with Hebrews 12:7-11

"Endure hardship as a discipline, God is treating you as a son. For what son is not disciplined by his father?" Hebrews 12:7-8

Here again hardship, and the Bible says it is a good thing.

God challenged me two more Bible verses. James 1:2 and 1 Peter 4:12-19.

"Consider it pure joy, my brothers, whenever you face trials of many kinds" ~ James 1-2

"Dear friends, do not be surprised at the painful trial you are suffering, as though something strange was happening to you." ~ 1 Peter 4 -12

Because I hate suffering, I really struggled and also wondered what God was telling me through these words. The last five years, I suffered tremendously from a sensitive nervous system. My legs tingled and I felt very uncomfortable for me to sit. I meditated on His words and almost memorized them.

After long meditations over these words, I started realizing that God is not telling me to suffer, but he wants to make me overcome through sufferings. He wants to develop perseverance, character, and hope in me. I really thanked God that he loves us so much that He changes us, teaches us, moulds us, and makes us into the likeness of His son Jesus. That is His purpose, not giving us a perfect and comfortable life. I really thanked God for His kind teaching. He changed my thinking and I realized that this is a new chapter in my life. A new season started, and a new chapter started. It took a long time, but it came to an end, at even my tingling stopped with medication my family doctor gave me.

The perennials are coming out already and promising a beautiful spring season. While I was enjoying my new spring season, I received a letter from Japan, Pastor Tanigawa at Mihara Lutheran Church, sent me a letter unexpectedly. He translated my book into Japanese and the church published a Japanese version of my book in 2014. That I knew, but he wrote that when he published my books, he sent a copy of Akemi's Journals to every Lutheran Church in Japan, and now one pastor from Nagano asked to have more books and to know my address. Pastor Tanigawa asked me if he could give this pastor my address. When I read his letter, I was shocked. I did not know Pastor Tanigawa sent a copy of my book to all the Lutheran churches in Japan. I don't even know how many Lutheran churches are in Japan. Are there 50 or 100 Lutheran churches in Japan? Every church received my book! I could not believe what Pastor Tanigawa did.

I said to God, "Father, what are you doing? I can't believe a copy of my book was sent to every Lutheran Church in Japan. You are so big, what you do is so huge I can't even think like that. Father, thank you, I am so honoured and blessed. Use my books for your glory in Japan and use me for your glory. This is truly an amazing life. I can live my life with you. Thank you, Father."

I sensed that God was smiling at me, and Isiah 55:8-9 came to my mind immediately.

"For my thoughts are not your thoughts,

neither are your ways my ways," declares the Lord.

"As the heavens are higher than the earth

So are my ways higher than your ways

 and my thoughts than your thoughts.

~ Isaiah 55: 8-9

I wrote a letter to Pastor Tanigawa that he can give my address to the pastor in Nagano Lutheran Church, so that he can contact me.

I really desire that the Japanese Christians come to know God's deep love for them and to be filled with joy knowing that they are deeply loved by the Heavenly Father, and they are so precious in God's eyes.

I continually pray for Salvation for Japan every morning, believing that my prayers work, and one day God will look at Japan and say, "It is good!"

13

You have a Public Speech

April 30, 2018

About a couple of months ago, Rita took Dianne and me to her church, Catch the Fire Toronto. We listened to the guest speaker's message. After the service, everybody received prayers from their ministry team members.

A lady came to me and said, "Akemi, good to see you."

The lady was Catherine, whom I met in a small group more than 20 years ago. She gave me a big hug and started praying, putting her right hand over my head. She blessed my life with Jesus, and when she finished her prayer she said, "You have a public speech to give. Bless you!" I thanked her and thought about a public speech. I spoke in front of 60 people at a book celebration gathering last December. I thought that Catherine was talking about that speech, but I kept it in my heart.

This winter, our church had a guest speaker to strengthen us and prepare us to be used by God. One Sunday, Pastor James declared that we will be used by God to spread the good news in Mississauga, even all over the world, because our church has many nationalities. If everyone prays for salvation for their own country, it is already a big job and pleases God. I was so excited to hear that message and said "yes!" in my heart.

After the service, I saw Pastor James was free, so I went to him and said, "Pastor James, I would like to tell you something."

"What would you like to tell me?" he asked.

I told him that when I published my book in 2012, I had sent three books to Japan, one for my sister, one for Pastor Asami, who baptized me, and one for my Christian friend who is a retired English teacher. These three can read English. Then my Christian friend, Hinako, took my book to her church, and her pastor read it, and he started using my book for a ladies' group, and one lady sent me a letter, and asked me for a Japanese version of my book, and if I did not have a Japanese one, she wanted to translate it and publish my book in Japanese. When I said yes, she paid half of the cost and the church paid the other half and they published my book in Japanese. That was three years ago. Recently I received a letter from Pastor Tanigawa who had translated my book. He wrote that when he published my book, he sent a copy of my book to every Lutheran church in Japan, and he is receiving responses now. One pastor from Nagano wanted to have more books and wanted to know my address.

Pastor James took both my hands and said, "This is awesome! You tell us this story next week." He thought a moment and said, "Next week is Easter, but it should be okay. Tell the people next week, okay?"

"Yes, I will," I said and went back to my chair.

I prepared my message in my mind, how to start, how to develop and how to finish, also to bring glory to God. I prepared it many times in the whole week and attended the Easter Sunday service.

On Easter Sunday we had so many people in our church. Many people came with their families and friends. Pastor James invited the people who had never believed in God to receive Jesus as their Savior and Lord. The service was so fruitful, and we truly celebrated the power of our resurrected Jesus. But we did not have time for my testimony.

At the end of the service, Pastor James said, "Akemi will tell us her story next Sunday." So I had another week to polish my testimony.

The following Sunday, on the 8th of April, Jeffrey and Suzanne drove me to our church. Soon the worship music started. We have wonderful musicians to lead our worship. I enjoyed singing worship songs to God. While I was singing, one of the leaders Ashisi, came to me and said, "Akemi, your testimony is right after the worship, okay?"

"Okay. How many minutes do I have, five or three?" I asked.

"We have 14 people to be baptized after your testimony."

"I'll try to make it as short as possible."

"Good. Thanks," he said and left.

Right after the worship, I was called to the front. Holding a microphone with my right hand, I started presenting my testimony.

"Good morning," I said and spoke to the people about my life of studying English as a second language and writing essays about the goodness of God in my life as homework. I told them how much writing about the goodness of God helped me to go through my life, because this trained my mind to look at something good in my life, instead of looking at problems. I also told them that I found the importance of giving thanks, because thanksgiving is the key to the Kingdom of God.

By coincidence, I published my book by meeting a teacher at a creative writing class at the Older Adult Centre, and I sent three books to Japan, one for my sister Sanae, Pastor Asami and my Christian friend Hinako, who is a retired English teacher. Hinako took my book to her church. Pastor Tanigawa used my book for a ladies' group and one lady asked me to publish it in Japan. When I said yes, they published it in Japanese. That was three years ago. Now I have found that when they published my books, Pastor Tanigawa sent a copy of my book to every Lutheran church in Japan, and now he has started receiving the results. One pastor from Nagano asked him to send more of my books and wanted to know my address.

I told the congregation that I was in awe of what had happened, because I had never expected this. I just wrote my essays as homework for my English lessons, and God did everything else. I emphasized how big our God is and how kind our God is. I told them, "Every time I came across difficulties in my life, I said to myself 'I have a problem now, but God knows what I am going through, and my God is bigger than this." I kept on saying how big God is, but I really didn't know just how big. I said to God, "God what are you doing? You are amazing," and He said to me, "Akemi, my daughter, you know that my ways are higher than your ways and my thoughts are higher than your thoughts." I thanked God and said, 'God use my books for your glory and use my life for your glory.' This is my testimony. Thank you."

The people applauded as I finished my testimony. There were almost 200 people there. I thought I would have difficulty making a public speech, but I did not. I rather enjoy telling the people about the goodness of God.

I truly thanked God for what I was able to do at our church and witnessed 14 people being baptized. I came home with great relief and a great satisfaction.

I remembered Catherine's prophecy, "Akemi, you will give a public speech." I realized that it was God's plan, and I thanked God for that.

14

I Visited Two Friends

May 13, 2018

In early May, I visited two older friends, Marlene Traas and Joe Wing-filder, who are very important people in my life. They have helped me so much and have encouraged me, and I am very thankful that I met them earlier in my life.

Marlene was a leader of a ladies Bible study group, and one day after we studied the Bible, she visited my house and baptized me with the Holy Spirit. When I lost my husband, she visited me and stayed overnight, and the next day she drove me to a Funeral Home to prepare my husband's funeral. I had to choose so many things very quickly, and I was overwhelmed to do such a job, and Marlene helped me in every step of the preparation.

She also typed my essays and put them in spiral-bound booklets. She called me often and asked me if I had enough essays to make booklets from my essays, and that helped me to publish my book.

Joe is a father of my good friend and trustee, Janis Flower. When I lost my husband, Joe and his wife Flo invited me often for dinner or a cup of tea in their backyard.

One day I was invited for an afternoon tea. I picked up their friend, Hazel, and drove there. While we were drinking a cup of tea in their beautiful backyard, suddenly the Holy Spirit hit me. I could not move and also I became so sleepy. Flo took me into their house, and I slept on the sofa for awhile.

Joe and Flo were so kind to me. Then Flo passed away. She moved to Heaven, and Joe developed dementia and he is living in Sunnybrook Hospital.

I was so excited to visit my wonderful friends that I painted two cards for them. On the 4th of May, Rita drove me to Marlene's condo in Oakville. When we arrived at the seniors' center, Marline opened the entrance door for us and welcomed us warmly. She invited us to her room on the 5th floor. She opened the door and said "Welcome, this is my room."

The room was quite a big room with a bed, two nice chairs, a big dresser, also a small fridge, stove and a sink, a quiet big bathroom and two closets, one a linen closet. As a senior's home, it is a luxury big condo, but compared to what she had before the size shrank so much. She used to live in a big house and moved to a big condo. After her husband died, she moved to a senior's home in Oakville and moved to Vancouver, and New Zealand. Now she has come back to Canada and I was so happy to meet her again!

Marlene sat on the edge of her bed and Rita and I sat on the comfortable chairs. We just talked. We talked of old times and also Marlene's experience in New Zealand. Soon teatime came, so we went down to the first floor. When Marlene got a cup of tea, we moved to a quiet place and sat on the chairs and talked continually.

Marlene looked a little older than before and could not remember many things, but she looked very happy and content. We came back to her room and Rita and I prayed over her. Marlene was so happy, and kept on saying, "Hallelujah, Hallelujah."

I was so pleased to see that Marlene does not own a big home anymore and she is losing her memory, but the spirit of God in her is so strong. It never leaves her. Even if everything changes, God's promise never changes. "Never will I leave you; Never will I forsake you." Heb 13:5. She will carry this glorious spirit until she goes home. I was so pleased that we visited Marlene. Rita drove me home, and I really thanked God for our visit.

The next day on the 5th of May, Janis Flower drove me to Sunnybrook Hospital to see her father, Joe Wingfilder.

When we arrived at the hospital, we went to the third floor. While we were walking towards his room, we found him in a wheelchair, and he was sleeping comfortably. When we said 'Hello,' Joe woke up and was surprised. He held my hand tightly and said, "Good to see you, Akemi." He was truly happy to be with us.

Janis wanted to take him to the beautiful flower gardens behind the building, but the garden was closed completely, because a strong wind had damaged the garden a few days ago. We decided to go to the front of the building, and we found a quiet place with a bench. Janis locked Joe's wheelchair beside the bench and let me sit next to Joe. He held my hand tightly again and said, "Akemi, thank you for coming. It is nice to see you." We looked at the trees and people walking and a big building in front of us, but it was very peaceful. I was very happy to sit with Joe.

After we talked awhile, I prayed over him for God's blessing for his future, and the wonderful life with God. Then Joe prayed over me for God's protection. In his prayer, Joe quoted many Bible verses. He remembered many Bible verses. I was so blessed. His prayer was so strong and alive. It was so beautiful, and the presence of God was so strong. I thanked God for his faithfulness. No matter what happens in our lives, His promises never change. Joe kept on saying "Glory to God, glory to God." What a beautiful life, because God is with him.

When our prayer time ended, suddenly heavy rain came down for a very short time, as if God opened the heavens and rain dropped. We were so excited about it.

I had a good time with Joe, and soon dinner time approached, so we sent Joe to the dining room and said, "Goodbye."

Joe shares the room with three men. He does not have a big room anymore and he is in a wheelchair. He can't move around by himself, but his relationship with God is getting bigger and stronger. Joe is smiling always, and he says "hi" to everyone he meets with a beautiful smile. God is smiling through him.

I was truly blessed these two days in a row in early May and thanked God for that. When I was talking about these two wonderful visits to my old friends, the Bible verse came to me.

"Who shall separate us from the love of God? Shall trouble or hardship or persecution or famine or nakedness or sword? …. no in all these things we are more than conquerors through Him who loved us." Romans 8:35-37

I sensed that I would experience more and more wonderful things in this year.

15

May the 27th

June 1, 2018

In April after the snow melted completely, my perennials started showing new shoots, but one night an ice storm hit and covered everything with ice again. My garden was covered in about 10 centimeters of ice pellets. We had a very uneasy April this year.

One afternoon, as I started watching TV, I saw the title 'hoarding' on the screen. A lady had accumulated so many goods in her house, so many boxes, clothes, ornaments, that she did not have space to put her foot down. Her house was full of goods everywhere. Soon she met a professional person to help her to solve her problem.

It was in the middle of the afternoon and I did not usually watch TV during the day. I knew I was wasting my time and I had lots of things to do in my house, but I could not stop watching the hoarding show. I sat on the chair and watched continually. Eventually, the lady got rid of lots of things even though it was very difficult for her, and made her house clean and roomy.

While I was watching hoarding, I could not stop watching and I felt so strange and asked God about it.

"Father, why am I so interested in this program and can't stop watching?" Then He told me, "Because it's very important to know spiritual hoarding."

"What?" I asked.

"Remember your body is a temple of God and the spirit of God lives in you."

"Yes, I do. He lives in me," I said.

"But when your desires, your plans, your goals are accumulated, your house is just like that."

I was shocked to hear that, and really thought about my temple. Am I using God to fulfill my plans, my desires, and my goals, or is he using me for his purpose?

On TV, the lady got a clean house and invited her children for dinner. When I finished watching TV, I was in awe, and thought about it a lot. I thought about a life truly surrendered to God would be so wonderful, so that the spirit of God can move freely in my life. In every situation, if I can pray "your will be done," instead of my will, and trusting fully that His way is better than my way. What kind of life it would be? I pondered about it for many days.

The ice melted completely, and the perennials started growing beautifully. I was so happy that I could look after the Lord's garden this year again. I am excited to take care of the garden. One day while I was reading the Bible Mark 8:34 spoke to my heart so strongly.

"If anyone would come after me, he must deny himself and take up his own cross and follow me."

I have read this many times before, but it did not speak much to me. But this time it hit me, as if Jesus was speaking to me. I thought Jesus wants me to die to myself so that he can live in me totally. What an awesome thought that was! I cherished it in my heart.

The month of May approached, and I started remembering the day my husband passed away. That was a beautiful Saturday, and the garden was filled with many flowers and the wisteria bloomed for the first time. I thought it was so strange that God wants me to die completely and I wanted to do that. It would be so nice if I declared my death on the 27th of May, the day my husband went to heaven. This year the 27th of May is on Sunday. I would have a memorial on May the 27th this year.

Suddenly my friend Rita called me in the afternoon of the 26th of May and wanted to visit me that evening. I was so happy to spend time with her. After supper Rita came and we talked. I mentioned what God was doing in my life recently, and we prayed together for our total surrender to him, and for the cleaning up of God's temple completely. It was so good and so suitable for the day of 26th of May.

The next day, I went to a church and saw Selina. I did not see her at the church for the last couple of weeks. We said good morning and hugged each other. Then Selina said that she and her daughter had attended a Christian conference in the USA for the last two weeks. She said, "It was so good."

"Oh, that's good. That's why I did not see you." Then I told her what God was telling me recently. I said, "I did not go to a conference, but God is telling me to die to myself." Then Selina said, "Oh Akemi, that was the theme of the conference."

"That's very interesting!"

Soon the service started. I truly enjoyed worshiping God, our Father, with my brothers and sisters. I had a very meaningful Sunday at the church.

When I came home and opened the living room door to go out, I saw the beautiful flowers blooming and wisteria blooming gently. It was exactly the same as the day Ken died. It has been 18 years since that day. I could not believe that I survived the last 18 years. God helped me so wonderfully well. Without His help I could not have made it.

I thanked God for that and also thanked God for my new chapter in the peaceful garden.

"Father, thank you for your help. You are so good. After 18 years of my husband's death, I am living with your joy and peace. What a wonderful gift I received from you! I'm so thankful to live my life with you. This is a wonderful life and an exciting life. Thank you, Father."

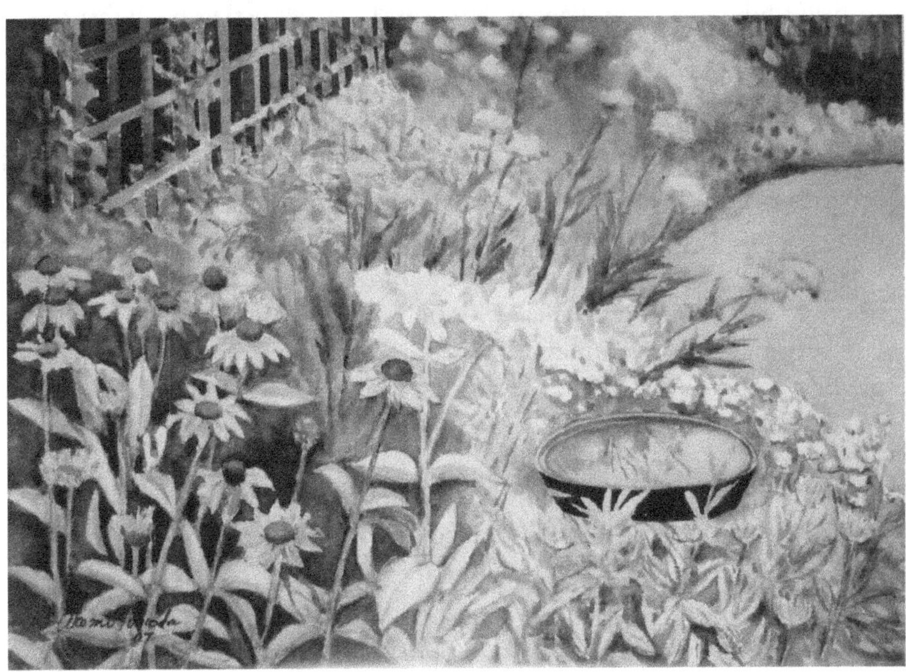

16

From the Garden

July 9, 2018

We have had strange weather this year. A few days of bitterly cold weather in April, and extremely hot days in May. We had about two weeks off unbelievably hot and humid weather in June. The temperature went up more than 35 degrees Celsius day after day and did not move. The strange weather affected the plants in the garden. Some perennials did not grow high, and some perennials took a long time to bloom.

Gradually the flowers started blooming and the Lord's garden was so beautiful and peaceful again this year. I started eating breakfast in the garden and I listened to God. I expected wonderful things would happen in the garden.

One morning, I was sitting on the sofa in the living room and reading the Bible. When I looked at the garden, I saw a robin standing on the garden table. I don't know why, but I watched it so intensely. The robin moved its wings very quickly. I felt so strange, but I did not know what it was. While I was watching the bird's movement, I found the robin was standing on one leg. The right leg was stuck to its body. It moved with difficulty and flew to the bird bath and stood on the edge of the bird bath with one leg. It drank water and bathed, but it looked so difficult. While I was watching the bird, I started praying for healing of the robin's leg very seriously. "In the name of Jesus and with His authority, I speak healing over your right leg. Healing, healing. I speak the healing of Jesus over you." I prayed so seriously for the bird from the living room. Then the robin started stretching out its right leg several times and drank water again and bathed one more time and flew away using the left leg only. I was so discouraged and said to myself, "one day it will work." This occurred of few weeks ago, and I forgot about the robin completely.

Yesterday, on the 8th of July, after I came home from church, I looked at the garden and saw the same robin on the bird bath again. The robin was standing at the edge of the bird bath on one leg, but this time it's right leg was stretched out 75%. It was still difficult for it to move around, but much better than before. I truly believed that this robin was the same robin I prayed over and thanked God for his healing over the little bird. This time the robin drank water and bathed and flew away beautifully.

I thanked God that he gave me the opportunity to look at that bird again, and thought this is the last time I will see that robin, because the next time it comes to the bird bath it will be using both legs. I looked at the garden with joy and thanksgiving in my heart. The garden was so peaceful!

I made a simple lunch and took it in the garden and ate it. Then Gary called me, "Hi Akemi, this is Gary I am coming around 3:00 o'clock. Is that okay?"

"Of course, it's okay. Thank you. Gary, can I ask you something?"

"Sure, what is it?"

"Could you remove a beehive?"

"Yes, I can. Where is it, in the front or at the back?"

"In the backyard."

"I will do that. See you soon."

My husband added a tiny roof at the back of the house over the living room door. Inside of the roof I found quite a big beehive. I did not know it was there until now. The beehive diameter was about 15 centimeters and many bees were going in and out of the beehive.

When Gary arrived, he wanted to get rid of the beehive before he cut the grass. He looked at the beehive and said, "It's so big. Akemi, did you not know that?"

"No, I did not."

I showed him a spray of insect killer, but he wanted to do it a different way. He took a bucket and cardboard and put the ladder under the beehive. He climbed up the ladder and covered the beehive with the bucket, then soon he screamed and jumped down the ladder and ran to the centre of the garden and got rid of the bees from his body frantically. The bees were attacking Gary.

"The bees are attacking me," Gary said.

"Oh no, Father help! Protect Gary from the bees," I said in my heart. I did not know what to do. Soon Gary said that he was stung in four places, forehead, right ear, neck, and arm.

"Would you like to see a doctor?" I asked.

Gary said, "No it's okay."

I kept on praying in my heart, "Help."

I felt so bad about this accident happening in the Lord's garden. It was really bad.

A little while later, Gary said, "I will cut the grass in the front and he took the electric cord and edge cutter and went to the front yard. He started cutting the edge and cut the grass and cleaned the front yard.

"Gary, are you okay?" I asked.

"I am okay. I am not allergic to bee stings."

After he finished the front, he used insect killer and sprayed the beehive heavily. Then soon some bees flew away and some bees started dropping on the ground. I stepped on each one of them. Eight bees dropped and the last one was a huge one. While Gary was cutting the grass in the back, I climbed up the ladder and removed the beehive with a shovel. It dropped on the ground. It was huge and there were so many larvae. I put it in the bucket and filled it with water."

When Gary finished cutting the grass, I offered him a cold drink. We sat on the garden chairs and relaxed. I asked him, "How are the bee stings? Are you alright?"

"I am okay," he said. He touched his forehead, ear and arm and said, "It's gone!"

I really thanked God for that.

Gary said that he had a little bump on his forehead, but the others had totally disappeared.

After Gary left, I truly thanked God for his healing over Gary's bee stings. Gary was stung by the bees in the Lord's garden, but God healed him in His garden.

The perennials are blooming beautifully, and I sensed God's peace in the garden. I will spend lots of time in this beautiful garden, this year too, and I thanked God for that.

17

In the Hot Summer

July 23, 2018

The summer of 2018 started with unusually hot weather. The temperature went up to 35 Degrees Celsius, with humidity over 40 degrees Celsius. This heat wave did not leave quickly, so we had a few weeks of very hot and uncomfortable days. I could not open the windows at all, and they reported that 53 people died in Québec. I believe many more people died from this heat wave.

One of those days, Shirley who lives across the street, called me. When I answered, she said, "Hi Akemi, this is Shirley. Can I ask you something?"

"Of course you can," I said.

Then she said, "Akemi, do you have air conditioning?"

"Yes, I do," I answered.

"Oh, I'm glad. It's hard to live without air conditioning nowadays."

"Thank you so much for asking me. I really appreciate your kindness," I said.

After Shirley's call, I thought if I did not have air conditioning, she would have invited me to her house to stay in a cool place. I thanked God for giving me such a wonderful neighbour on our street.

This was the first summer I had to live life without a car. I had to make good plans to do my shopping by using a bus. I wanted to be independent, so I decided to go shopping at least once a week, taking the 9:15 bus and returning home before 10:30. I had to make a good shopping list, and I did well. I did not have any problems. I truly thanked God for that.

But also many friends helped me with my grocery shopping too.

Janette and her husband, Ben, took me out for shopping. They took me to Costco and Longo's, and I did some good shopping. They said that they were moving to Georgetown to live with their daughter and her family. At the last minute, they found time and helped me. I was so thankful for their help.

They helped me to clear the snow on my driveway in the winter of 2017, when I suffered from some knee pain. I was able to go through that winter. I really thanked them for their kindness.

While we were coming home from shopping, Janette asked me, "Akemi, where do you take a bus? Do you walk to Winston Churchill?"

"No at the entrance of our street," I said.

"At Winwood and Townwood?"

"Yes, I walk a little bit."

"That's so amazing! Akemi, God knew you needed a bus," she said.

I never thought that way, but it is so easy to take a bus from a street. I don't have to walk a long distance. I thank God in my heart for His wonderful provision, and also Janette and Ben for their kind help. I was so blessed to know them. In a couple of weeks, they moved to Georgetown.

In this hot summer, many of my friends helped me grocery shopping.

Rita helped me many times. One day she took me to Oakville, and we did grocery shopping at an organic grocery store. I enjoyed shopping there and picked up many things. One day she took me to Costco. I bought two pots of perennials for my garden. It was fun and I thanked her. One day she drove me to Shoppers Drug Mart and Freshco. She helped me a lot in this hot weather and I really thanked her for her kindness. I said to God, "Lord I am so blessed to have such wonderful friends in my life. Thank you so much. Bless them abundantly."

I tried to do shopping by taking a bus regularly. One morning, while I was waiting for a bus, I realized that the place I was waiting was a shady place, because of the big tree at the corner house. It was a very hot day, and I was so pleased to stand in the shade of the big tree. It reminded me of Jonah when God provided shade for him. I said in my heart, "Did you plant this tree for me so that I can wait for a bus comfortably? Thank you so much. I am very comfortable." Soon a bus came and I went shopping.

God sent me so many wonderful friends to help me. On the 19th of July, suddenly my friend Carol called me and wanted to visit me. We decided to see each other in the afternoon of that day. Before Carol visited me, she called me again and said, "Akemi, I would like to come and see you now. Do you need something? I can pick up for you at Freshco?"

I said, "Carol, could you take me to Freshco after your visit?"

"Of course, I can do that. Okay, let's do that."

She came, we spent time together in the garden where the perennials were blooming gorgeously, and God joined us. After her visit, she drove me to Freshco and drove me home.

Carol said to me, "My husband said, if you need a ride, let us know. We can help you in this hot weather."

I really thanked her and her family.

The next day on the 20th of July, I had a call from my publisher, Cheryl, unexpectedly. She said, "Hi Akemi, this is Cheryl. I would like to visit you. Can I come in 10 minutes? I have a cheque for you from Amazon."

"Of course, you can come," I said. She arrived soon and gave me a cheque. I was shocked. My book had sold. I could not believe it.

Cheryl said, "Do you need any grocery shopping? I can take you."

"Thank you. I am okay now," I said.

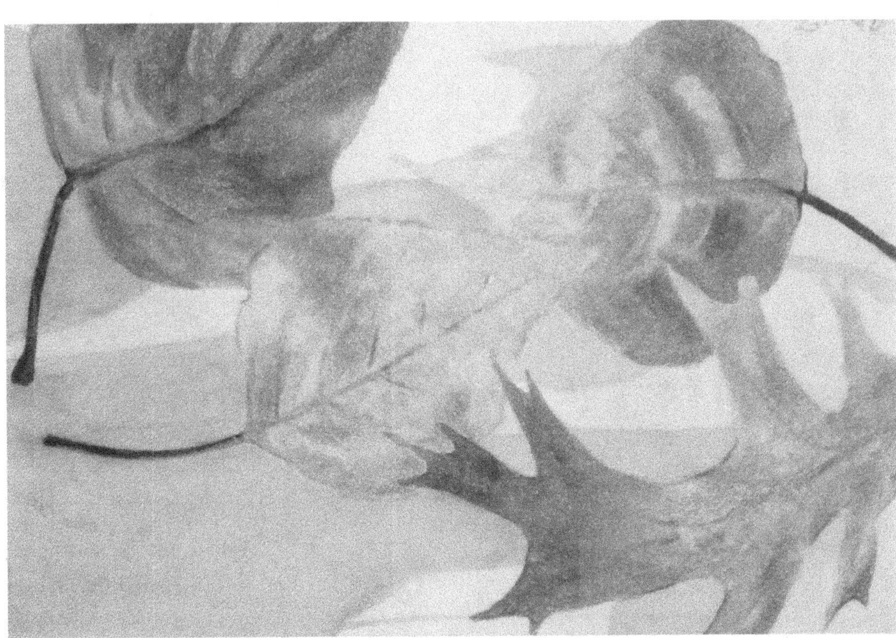

She said, "If you need a ride to your church, let me know. I can drive you. It's important for you to attend a church, right?"

"Yes, thank you so much for your offer, but my friends drive me there," I said.

She said, "If you need to go anywhere, let me know. I live very close to you."

"Thank you, you are so kind." I gave her a big hug.

Then the following day on the 21st of July at 9:00 o'clock, my friend, Chintsu called me and said, "Akemi, this is Chintsu. I would like to take you shopping. Where would you like to go? Nations? TNT? Wherever you want to go, I can take you."

"Thank you, Chintsu, I haven't eaten breakfast yet. If you can come at 10:30, I would like to go with you."

"Okay, I will be there at 10:30."

I ate breakfast very quickly and read the Bible. I did an exercise in the basement, and I was ready. Chintsu drove me to Freshco. I had shopped only two days ago, yet I picked up some items and I was very happy. I had enough fruits and veggies for awhile. She drove me home and went out in the garden and enjoyed the flowers.

I really thanked God for my wonderful friends he has sent to me in my life. He surrounds me with kind people who have helped me tremendously in this hot summer!

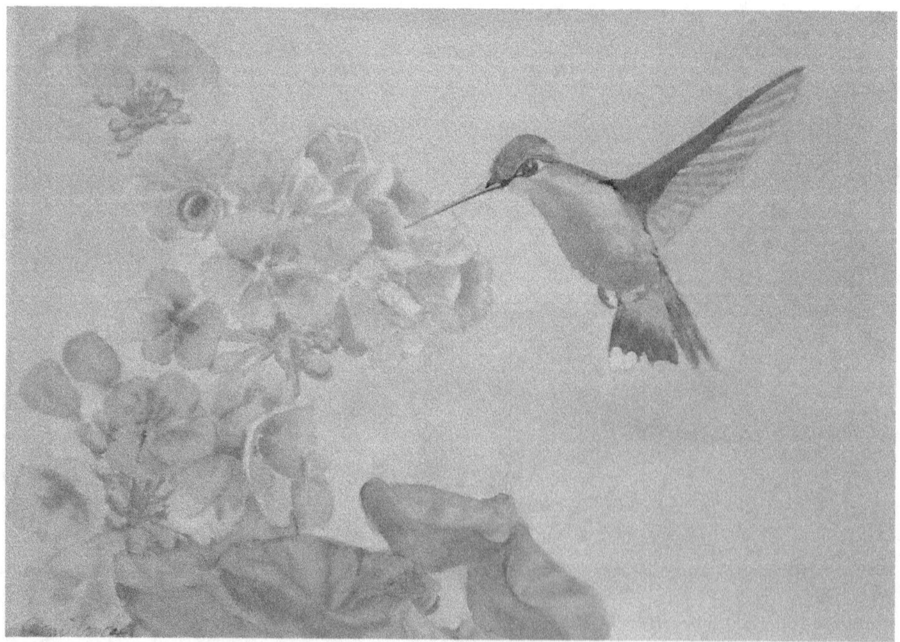

18

Prayer Night in the Hot Summer

August 10, 2018

When hot summer continued, and this unusually hot weather has brought many disasters. People have died from the heat, and fire has spread in the forests and burned many houses. It's not only in Canada, but all over the world.

One day in July, my friend Sayomi called me from Japan and told me that Japan had experienced some torrential rain for a few days, and many places were soaking in water. Sayomi said many places in Hiroshima were underwater, and worried about my sister Sanae, who lives very close to her Hiroshima. She asked me for Sanae's phone number, and I gave it to her.

Soon I called Sanae and I found out that her house was safe. Sanae said, "Because my house is built on the hill, we are safe, but very close to my house in Hiroshima is under water, and people are evacuated."

Sanae also told me about my husband, Ken's sister in Mihara. I called Fusako and found out her house was safe, but many houses are under water. She has electricity but does not have water." Sanae mentioned that the trains were not moving anymore. After I had talked to Sanae, I felt so sad.

A few days later, when I was coming home from grocery shopping, I talked to a lady who lives across the street. She said she is from Romania and Romania has had very heavy rain and the people were suffering from that.

When I heard so much bad news, I felt heaviness in my heart and wanted to pray for that. Not only heavy rain and soaking in the water but also fire in Canada and the USA. Fire is destroying the forests and houses. One night I watched TV and saw the whole globe was covered with very hot heat.

"Oh God, help us and forgive us," I said in my heart. Is this a judgment or what? I thought to myself, but I did not have any idea about it. I did not know what it was, but I knew that I had to pray for that.

The next morning I sat on the sofa in the living room, watching the beautiful flower garden and prayed to God asking for forgiveness for selfishness and asked God for our own purpose as Christians instead of asking for His perfect will be done on earth. I confessed my sins as a child of God and asked for forgiveness. I finished my prayer, but I knew that I had to pray more. I said to God, "I would like to pray more about this matter with somebody. Could you send me a prayer partner? I asked in Jesus' name. Amen."

Since then, one Sunday at our church, I talked to one lady about this matter, but she said, "It's not work. It's already happening. We can ask for His help for the people who are suffering." It did not work.

Then soon my old friend called me and asked me our mutual friend's address and phone number. After I gave her the address and phone number, I asked about the natural disasters all over the world and said "I sense we have to pray about it. What do you think?"

She said immediately "Yes we do."

"Could we pray together?" I asked.

"Yes, we can. Akemi, I will visit you one day," she said.

It was very nice, but she lives in Oakville and we all have busy lives. I did not hear from her.

So many people were killed in Toronto without any reason, and we had extremely hot weather and such heavy rain. This is the pattern of this summer.

On the 4th of August, I was busy with altering my friend's clothes until 5:30 PM. When I finished the alteration, I wanted to prepare my dinner. Then Sayomi called me from Japan and talked to me until 6:00 o'clock. When I said, "goodbye" to Sayomi, the phone rang again, and it was Rita. She wanted to visit me that evening and spend time with me. I said, "yes" to her, and thought can I prepare a dinner and eat and water the garden in one and a half hours?

Soon I started preparing supper and at the same time I started the sprinkler in the backyard. I checked the time and moved the sprinkler to a different place. I ate supper and called Rita and said, "Rita, when you come, please enter my house since the entrance door is unlocked, I might be watering in the backyard."

Then I watered the flowers and vegetables gently with the sprayer.

Soon Rita came and walked into my house. We sat on the sofa in the living room as usual, watching the flower garden with a cup of tea. I mentioned about my feelings towards the natural disasters all over the world and asked, "Rita, do you think these things happening all over the world is God's judgment?"

She said, "I don't know whether it's judgment or not, but I think it's a warning."

"Do you think we can pray and ask forgiveness from God?" I asked.

"Sure, we can do that. It's a good idea. You are Japanese, you can ask forgiveness for the Japanese people, and I can ask forgiveness for Quebec, and we can ask forgiveness for Canada, and we are Christians, so we can do it for the body of Christ."

Then we really prayed, confessing our sins and asked for forgiveness. I prayed for Japan, for our pride, that we think we can live our lives without God. Even God sent many missionaries to Japan. We don't pay any attention to that. Rita prayed for Québec and Canada. We also asked forgiveness for the body of Christ, not asking His will but asking our desires and our plans to be fulfilled. We started praying, while we were able to see the flowers in the garden and finished our prayer when it was pitch dark outside.

When our prayer ended, I felt such a strong anointing coming over me. We spent more time with the Holy Spirit. I started feeling lighter in my heart. The heaviness was gone. I truly thanked God for giving me a prayer partner and the time to pray together. We had a wonderful time with the Lord.

When Rita was going home, she said, "I am glad I came."

I said, "I am so happy we were able to pray tonight."

Then Rita said, "I am glad I did not listen to the flesh. I was kind of tired."

I said, "Me to."

I had quite a busy day and I had to water the garden, but everything went well, and I thanked God for using us for his purpose.

19

I Attended a Bridal Shower

September 15, 2018

I was invited to a bridal shower for Jenna Hay, daughter of my friend Carol Hay, on the 6th of September. My friend Maria and her daughter Angelica drove me to a nice condo in the south of Mississauga near the lake.

When we arrived, we were welcomed by two ladies and invited to a gathering room. The room was decorated beautifully, and seven tables were prepared. Each table was covered with a white tablecloth and decorated elegantly with teacups and saucers, and four chairs for each table.

We arrived there very early, but soon other ladies started coming. About 30 ladies got together with gifts and enjoyed a very special gathering for Jenna.

I saw some old friends, and it made me so happy. We had studied the Bible together with some of the ladies and with some ladies we had prayed together. It was so wonderful to see them!

We had good food and interesting games and the time went by so quickly. In one game, we had to pick up one earring from an earring case and find the person who had the same earring, and then sit together as partners. I picked a big pearl earring and looked for the matching earring and found Jenna. We hugged each other and I said, "Congratulation, Jenna."

"Thank you, Akemi. You know I miss my grandmother so badly at a time like this," Jenna said.

"I miss her too," I said.

Jenna's grandmother, Flo Wingfilder, is in Heaven now and she is smiling at her granddaughter now. Flo was such a kind lady and she helped me a lot after I lost my husband. At her backyard, while we were having a cup of tea one afternoon, the Holy Spirit hit me so strongly that I had to take a nap at her house for awhile. It was already 18 years ago, but I still remember it so clearly.

Jenna and I sat together, and Angelica and another lady sat together at our table. We played a game and talked to each other. Then a lady in front of me suddenly said, "Akemi, good to see you. Do you remember me?"

I looked at her, but I did not remember her at all. I said honestly, "I am sorry. I don't remember you."

Then the lady said, "I am Sharon. I am a friend of Janis. I met you at Tim Horton's one day about five years ago." Suddenly I remembered her. One evening Janis took me to Tim Horton's in Streetsville to meet her friend to buy a turkey. I said, "Yes, I remember you. How are you?"

"I am okay. How are you doing?" she asked me.

"I am good. Thank you," I said, and added. "I am content."

Then Sharon said, "Yes, I can see. It's not just words. I can see you are good."

"Yes I am. I'm very thankful for that."

We continued our game, and it was fun!

We had to come home before the gifts were opened, because Maria had to come home early. I enjoyed the shower and enjoyed talking to Sharon at the same table.

When Maria drove me home, I really thanked God for the shower I had attended and thought about the last five years.

About five years ago, I started having a problem with my nervous system. My nervous system started tingling so badly. I prayed and prayed. I asked many friends to pray for me. I went to see the specialist and took an MRI for my brain, neck, and spine. They could not find the reason, and I just suffered. Meanwhile, I found out that certain foods affect my nervous system badly. I could not eat so many things. I could not go to any restaurant, and also, I could not take any trips. I was housebound and cooked my own meals for the last five years. I could not go on any journey. They were out of my life completely.

It was very difficult and also depressing. In spite of all these problems, I was able to have one journey. This journey was a special journey to the heart of God. I took this journey very seriously and also enjoyed it very much.

I talked to God a lot and also listened to him a lot. I started seeking His purpose for my life, instead of seeking my purpose. I also came to know God's huge love for his children. I am so grateful for that and I truly believe that the last five years of my journey to the heart of God was so meaningful for my life, and I don't want to exchange it for anything.

I came to the point that I love ordinary things I do every day, because I do everything with God. I started thanking God for the wonderful life with God.

I thanked God that I was able to attend Jenna's bridal shower and to meet Sharon again. She saw the difference in me.

The next afternoon, Janis Flowers called me and told me about the bridal shower. She said, "Akemi, I'm so sorry you had to go home before we opened the gifts. When Jenna opened your gift, everybody was surprised. I told them you painted that picture, and because Jenna's marriage is in the fall, you gave her a fall picture. I also told her that you made a bag too. Thank you so much."

"Thank you for telling me Janis," I said.

I gave Jenna a very peaceful fall landscape, which I painted from a park in Oakville. A few red trees were in the background, and a wide field with two tiny herons. It was a very peaceful painting. I truly hoped that Jenna and Phillip's new life will be a peaceful one, and they will be together in their fall season. I prayed to God for his special blessings for their marriage.

I was so blessed to attend the bridal shower and I thanked God for that special day.

20

The Fall of 2018

October 17, 2018

In the middle of September, my friend Sayomi called me from Japan, and told me that she was planning to visit the USA and Canada. She asked me, "Is it okay to visit you in the fall?"

"Of course, I have your room in my house. Come and visit me. Let me know when you can come," I said.

Since then I did not hear from Sayomi for two weeks. The last week of September, Sayomi called me and said, "I will be in Buffalo on the 28th of September. I will rent a car and drive to visit you on the morning of the 29th."

"Alright, see you soon."

I prepared the guest room.

Sayomi arrived safely on the morning of September the 29th. She brought lots of gifts from Japan, and we talked a lot.

The weather was comfortable and Sayomi drove me many places so that I was able to do shopping. She helped me to cut the bridal wreath at both sides of my backyard. I really thanked her for her help. I asked God what to pray for her during her stay, and whatever I received from God, I took time and prayed over her. We really had a good time together, and I thanked God for that.

While we were cooking together and eating together, we talked a lot. One day Sayomi said, "Akemi, you look healthier than before and also look younger."

I thanked her for her comment and also thanked God for His healing power over me. I was able to enjoy Sayomi's stay for a week. I prayed over Sayomi a lot, and I even invited my good friend Rita to pray over Sayomi one night. Rita came in the evening of the 4th of

October, and prayed over Sayomi. Sayomi was very happy to receive Rita's prayer.

After the prayer, Rita said, "We have Joshua Mills tomorrow night at our church. Let's go together. It's good for you, Sayomi." So we decided to go to Catch the Fire Toronto the following day.

On the next day, Rita came a little after 7, and drove Sayomi and me to Dianne's house and we went to CTF Toronto. We had good worship and the guest speaker, Joshua Mills, spoke. He talked about glory. He said glory to God and God is glory, and we can approach God through only thanksgiving. That really encouraged me. I thought I would continue my life of thanksgiving. He taught a lot, but when he started speaking in tongues, I felt the atmosphere changed, and after he spoke in tongues, he started singing in tongues. It was so beautiful! I was in awe, and truly enjoyed being there.

Joshua Mills sang quite a long time in tongues and the meeting ended. I was so happy that I had gone there.

Rita drove us home. When we arrived at home it was close to 11:00 PM.

The next day Sayomi and I ate breakfast, and I made sandwiches and cut fruit for Sayomi's lunch. Sayomi left around 11:00 o'clock. I prayed to God for Sayomi's safe drive and His blessing on her stay in the USA. I really thanked God that I was able to have Sayomi for a week and was able to cook for her.

In the afternoon while I was vacuuming the living room, I realized that I was singing. I did not know what I was singing, but soon I noticed that I was singing in tongues. I stopped the vacuum cleaner and listened to my singing. It was so beautiful, and my heart was filled with God's peace. I was truly in awe and thanked God for opening a new world for me. I felt so good all day, and since then thankfulness in my heart increased. I just enjoy being a child of God immensely with singing.

A week later, the 12th of October, Rita took Dianne and me to CTF Toronto again, and we had Joshua Mills as a speaker again. After wonderful worship, Joshua spoke about the glory again. This time he taught us about three steps in a faith journey, believe, anointing, and glory. He invited all of us to get into the glory realm, and each one of us was prayed over. It was so wonderful. I really thanked God for what I experienced that night. We came home late again, but I was so happy that I was able to listen to Joshua's teaching for two Friday nights.

On the 14th of October, I prepared myself to go to church. While I was reading the Bible, two Corinthians 3:17-18 came to me strongly:

"Now the Lord is the spirit, and where the spirit of the Lord is, there is freedom. And we, who with unveiled faces all reflect the Lord's glory and being transformed into his likeness with ever increasing glory, which comes from the Lord, who is the spirit." ~ 2 Corinthians 3:17-18

When I read these verses, I said to God, "Lord are you giving these words to me? It's awesome!"

I meditated on it for a long time, and my heart was full of joy and thanksgiving. I sensed a new season was starting in my life, and I said in my heart:

"Thank you, Father. You are so good. You are so kind. Thank you for creating me and taking me into your family, and blessing me. This is the best birthday gift from my heavenly Father. I received it with thanksgiving. I turned 81 today. I never thought I would be able to live this long before I met Jesus. Thank you so much!"

I spent a good time with the Lord this morning. Then suddenly the telephone rang. When I answered the phone, a lady started singing: "Happy birthday to you. Happy birthday to you. Happy birthday, dear Akemi. Happy birthday to you."

It was my friend Ingrid from Germany.

"Thank you, Ingrid. You are so kind," I said.

"I wanted to call you before you go to church. Akemi, have a wonderful day. God bless you!"

I really thanked her and also God for giving me wonderful friends in my life. I started my 81st year with wonderful blessings beginning on my birthday October 14.

21

The Peaceful Fall

November 19, 2018

One day in September, while I was cleaning my bookcase, I found an old calendar from the Canadian Red Cross. It was called "Landscape 2015 Calendar." I looked at the cover of the calendar and I could not throw it away. It was so beautiful with a few boats on the blue water and a few cottages and autumn red trees under a blue sky. The water reflected the shapes of the boats and the cottages intricately. I looked at the picture for awhile and wanted to paint the beautiful water so badly. The water moved with many reflections of different colours.

I stopped cleaning immediately and took out my watercolour paper and pencil and I started sketching the beautiful lake very quickly. I took out my palette and brushes. I mixed the watercolour paint and started painting the sky, then the red leaves of the fall trees, the cottage, and the water with the reflection of the boats, and the movement of the water. I was totally immersed in painting and I enjoyed it very much.

I usually attend art classes in the fall, but this year I could not do that because I don't drive anymore. I painted the landscape of the lake and I enjoyed it so much. I thanked God for the time I spent painting. I sensed such peace in my heart.

When I completed the painting, I cut the mat to the right size and attached it to my painting and put it in a plastic bag. It was ready to be framed, and I put this landscape on a little cabinet in the guest room.

After a couple of weeks, my friend Salem visited me. When I told her what I was doing recently, and showed her my new painting, she said, "Can I have it? I like it very much."

I said, "The sketch is not accurate. If you need one, I can paint one for you."

I showed her the pole on a boat and the reflection of the pole on the water which were not correct.

Then she said, "I don't see it, but if you paint one for me, I will be happy. Thank you, Akemi."

So I painted one for Salem, the same landscape with accurate drawing. I enjoyed painting it so much and I was so content. When I completed it, I cut the mat and framed it for Salem.

At the end of September, I had a visitor from Japan. Sayomi visited me and stayed at my house for a week. When she saw my new painting, she said, "I like the painting very much. Can I have it?"

"No, I painted this picture for Salem. I can't give it to you," I said.

Then she said, "How about another one?" She was pointing to the first one I painted.

When I told her that the sketch wasn't accurate, she said, "It doesn't matter at all. I like it. Can I have it?"

"Okay, if you don't mind, it's yours."

Sayomi was happy. When she left my house, she took three more of my watercolour paintings with her.

When Salem visited me the next time, I gave her the nicely framed painting of the landscape.

After I gave my painting to Sayomi and Salem, I did not have any lake landscapes and I missed them so much that I painted one more for myself. This was already the third time I painted the same thing, but I truly enjoyed the watercolor painting, mixing the colour, and adding the water. I had a good time and a very peaceful time at my house. I really thanked God for the way I was spending my time in the fall.

I had a good time in the garden this fall too. Because we had such hot summer, some flowers did not bloom until the middle of fall, so this fall the garden was full of flowers and I enjoyed it so much. We also had enough rain so that I did not have to water at all. When November came, the weather pattern changed swiftly. It became so cold like winter had arrived.

I started cleaning the garden a little by little, cutting the perennials. Then we had a couple of very windy days, that scattered lots of maple leaves and seeds from my neighbour.

I checked the weather forecast and decided to clean my backyard on the 12th of November in the afternoon. It wasn't raining and the morning was cold, but by the afternoon the temperature went up to 7 degrees Celsius.

In the morning of 12th of November, when I checked outside, I saw my next-door neighbour Erwin already cleaning his backyard. He was raking with a rake so neatly, and already half was done, piling up the leaves here and there. I also saw Erwin's next-door neighbour Sean was using a lawn mower picking up all the leaves into the lawnmower bag. I thought that was a very smart idea. Then suddenly I wanted to clean my backyard too. I went out and started using an electric blower. I moved the leaves from the flower garden to the centre of the yard. It was quite heavy, and I had never used it before, only Gary had used it regularly. Somehow, I managed to blow the leaves to the centre of the yard. Then I raked with a rake and put them into yard waste bags. I could not pick up lots of the maple seeds, so I used a lawn mower and cleaned my backyard so neatly. When I finished cleaning, I was so happy and thanked God for what I had accomplished. I am still able to look after his garden and was able to clean it. I had such joy and peace in my heart.

When I finished the cleaning, I took five-yard waste bags out and I came into the house. Then soon the telephone rang. It was UPS. A lady told me that my 17 calendars were ready to be picked up. I thanked her for a very quick job.

I checked the bus schedule and I had 15 minutes. I ate lunch in five minutes and prepared myself and went out to take a bus. The bus came soon, and I was in the bus alone as no one was in the bus. Soon I arrived at Meadowvale Town Centre and went to UPS and received 17 of my new 2019 calendars. I put them in my buggy, and I took a bus and came home.

When I arrived home, I took my new calendars into the living room and put them on the table. I put my hands over the calendars and thanked God for the calendars.

I was able to look after the Lord's garden this year again and was able to take photos from the garden and make calendars. Without His help I could not have done this. I also prayed for His blessings over my friends who will receive these calendars. I asked God to bless my friends every month of the year in 2019. My heart was full of joy and peace from God.

I did everything I do every year, but this year I did everything with such joy and thanksgiving and also peace. I was surrounded by such peace like I never experienced in my life. I was very thankful for this experience and I realized that I just started knowing God's huge love little by little through my ordinary life.

I am very grateful to be a child of God and I belong to His family.

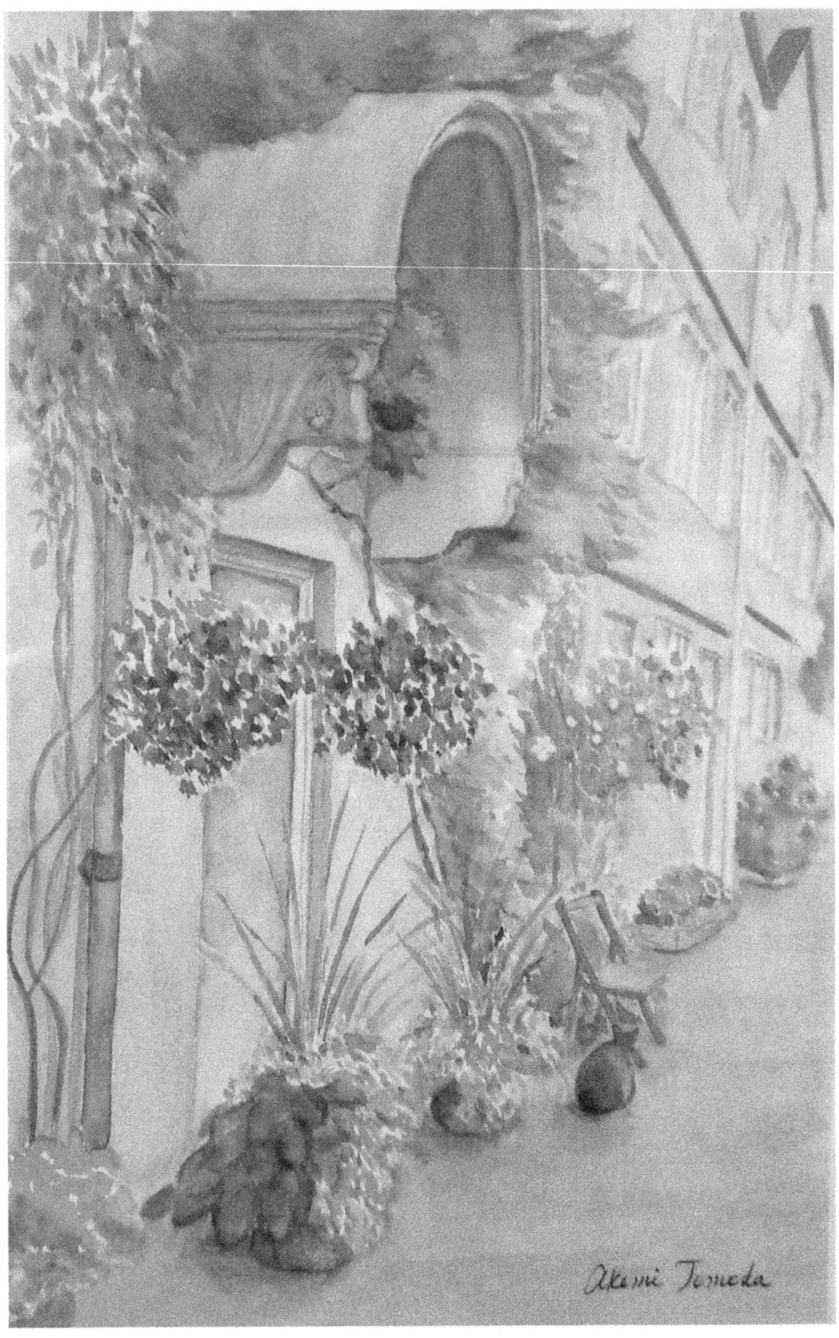

22

Thank You for a Wonderful Year

December 15, 2018

Christmas decorations are in the living room, and a huge pot of poinsettia from Daniel added more Christmas colour in the room. The light on the Christmas tree were shining beautifully, and the Hallelujah chorus from Handel's Messiah is in the air. The season of celebrations has started. I have already received a few Christmas cards from my friends.

Sitting on the sofa in the living room, I looked at the empty garden. The garden is cleaned so neatly, and it will be covered by snow soon. This is the time for it to rest until the next spring.

Surrounded by Christmas decorations, I looked back over the year 2018, and thanked God for His kindness for every season.

In the spring, when the perennials started growing, I watered the garden for the first time, and saw a double rainbow in the air. I was so excited and thanked God for that.

"Thank you, Father, the double rainbow is here again. Your presence is here. I will have a beautiful time in your garden again this year."

While the grass started growing, Gary came to cut the grass again this year. He has been helping me already for 18 years. He has helped me in so many ways and made my life so safe. I thanked God for his kindness and his faithfulness.

Spring flowers started blooming, and I started eating my breakfast in the garden. I talked to God and listened to Him a lot surrounded by spring flowers. I truly had a beautiful time in His garden.

This summer was a very hot summer and the plants struggled to grow. The summer flowers did not bloom until late summer. We had lots of rain so that I did not have to water often.

Our ladies Bible study continued in my living room through the summer, and the ladies enjoyed the garden. Elli led our Bible study and Dianne, Janette, Rita, and I studied the book of Revelations seriously, and encouraged each other. Lots of thanksgiving and praises went to heaven from my living room this summer again. I am very thankful for that.

Eventually the summer flowers started blooming and they lasted for quite a long time. I enjoyed these gorgeous summer flowers.

After a long hot summer day, suddenly very cold days came. I started cleaning the garden. Little by little I cleaned up the garden, and I truly thanked God for giving me good health, so that I was able to clean the garden by myself.

Fall came. One day in November I called my sister-in-law, Yaye in Thunder Bay. She turned 100 years this summer, and she is living in a nursing home. While I talked with her, she sounded so tired and her voice was so weak. I had a hard time hearing.

She said, "I can't go to the washroom by myself now. I need help to get up and move."

I felt so sad to hear that.

"I am sorry," I said.

Then she continued, "I don't want to stay here. I asked Ken to come and take me home with him, but he never came."

Ken is my husband, who went to Heaven 18 years ago. I said, "I know, we can't do anything about it. Only God decides how long we live."

After our conversation, the thought came to me so strongly that Yaye needs to receive Jesus officially. She was a Buddhist, and I prayed for her salvation every morning for more than 30 years. The last year, she said to me, "I thank God every morning and every night."

When Rita visited me, we prayed together, and I mentioned about Yaye. Then Rita prayed for her salvation. Rita prayed for a clear mind for Yaye and courage for me.

The following week on the 15th of November, I sensed that I had to call Yaye, so I called and she answered clearly. After we talked awhile, I said, "You know when we die there are two places to go, heaven and hell, if we want to go to heaven, we must have Jesus in our lives. Would you like to invite Jesus into your life? I would like to pray to invite Jesus into your life. Can you repeat this prayer?"

Then she said, "Yes, I will."

I was so pleased and prayed the Sinner's Prayer from the beginning to the end. She repeated so clearly, and when we said "Amen," Yaye said, "Thank you, you are so kind to me."

I was so happy and thanked God from the bottom of my heart. I have prayed for Yaye's salvation every morning for more than 30 years, but my prayers weren't wasted. I was so encouraged. What a fruitful fall! I could not stop thanking God.

The year 2018 is passing by so soon. When I look back over this whole year, I received so much help from so many people, and I thanked God for that.

Rita drove me to grocery shopping often and helped me a lot, specially in the hot summer. It was so comfortable, and I thanked God for that.

Chintsu also took me out for grocery shopping often and we prayed together in her car. I really thanked God for her help in spite of her busy life.

Jeffrey and Suzanne gave me a ride to our church every Sunday. They gave me such peace in my life, and I am very thankful for that.

Widad drove me to her house and took care of my hair and drove me back to my house. I thanked God for her kindness.

My trustees, Gary and Janis helped me a lot as usual and I thanked God for that too.

I truly thanked God for surrounding me with wonderful people who have helped me all the year. I thanked God for His kind help through my life, His protection, His provision, His mercy, His grace. I am overwhelmed by His goodness. The most wonderful thing is that He is with me and He is in me. "Emanuel" God is with us. I would like to celebrate this reality. "What a wonderful life! What a precious life! Thank you, Lord. You are with me."

The seasonal celebration is here. I would like to celebrate the birth of Jesus with lots of thanksgiving.

23

I Received Two Books from Japan

December 29, 2018

One day in early December, my sister, Sanae called me from Japan and told me that she had sent me two books. I did not understand what she was saying, so I asked, "What kind of books?"

Then she said, "Art books. Shigeru Nomura's watercolour books. The other day, I said to Shigeru that I feel so sorry for Akemi. She can't attend art classes anymore because she does not drive any more. Then Shigeru said, 'Let's buy art books and send them to her.' So, we bought two books and sent them to you."

"Thank you, so much. You are so kind." I was really stunned by their thoughtfulness.

Then Sanae said, "This artist, Shigeru Nomura's style is different from yours, so if you don't like it, you don't have to paint his style. Okay?"

"Sure, thank you. I really appreciate your kindness."

Within 10 days, the two books arrived. The Canadian Postal rotating strike was now over, and parcels were arriving smoothly. When I opened the books, very soft Japanese style watercolours appeared. One book is how to draw, and the other book is showing how to paint step by step, Shigeru Nomura's art class, from pencil drawing to painting with watercolours. There are four different landscapes from spring to winter.

I enjoyed watching his paintings and also enjoyed reading about his teaching. His paintings are so different from what I learned here in Canada. Shigeru's painting with pencil drawing is so precise and almost completed by pencil, and even draws shadows by pencil, and afterwards completes the pencil drawing using very soft and transparent watercolours lightly. They look like the Japanese world.

I wanted to try his style of painting and started painting cherry blossoms on a very small paper. The paper was covered with cherry blossoms and a tiny church tower was on top of the flowers. I drew the tower very precisely with a pencil and even the flowers with pencil drawing and putting the colour in Shigeru's style. I enjoyed painting and also learned the different way of painting.

The next day I had a little time and painted a full season of red Japanese maple branches. I enjoyed learning the new technique.

In a couple of days, I painted summer and winter seasons on very small papers with green trees and a snow-covered tree. I also painted a little bird sitting on a small snow-covered branch of red berries for Shigeru's birthday. I put my four paintings in an envelope with a thank you note, and Shigeru birthday card in a different envelope.

The next day on the 18th of December, I walked to the mailbox near my house. It took only three minutes to get there. I am so thankful for that every time I post any email. I put two envelopes into the mailbox and walked home. It was quite cold, but I was so happy that I had accomplished it.

Exactly 10 days later, on the 28th of December, when I was relaxing after supper, Sanae called me. She said "Thank you. We received all the cards you sent us."

"You're welcome. So, every card arrived safely? That's nice."

"Yesterday morning we received your cards and in the afternoon we went out for shopping and bought small frames and framed them all."

"Already? Thank you for sending me those books. I'm enjoying them very much."

"Shigeru said she can paint!"

"Thank you. Did you receive Shigeru birthday card too?"

"Yes, it's already framed."

I told Sanae that I am enjoying painting in Japanese style and I can paint anytime at my home. Also while a painting is drying, I can do so many things at home, cleaning, cooking, anything and I can come back and paint.

I really thanked my sister and her husband for their thoughtful kind hearts, because I never said to anyone that I missed art classes or I feel so sad that I can't attend art classes. Their kindness touched me deeply and I thanked God for my kind sister Sanae and her husband

Shigeru. I also thanked God for surrounding me with beautiful kind people. What a blessing I have received!

Two more days until the new year of 2019. I can close this year with a heartfelt thanksgiving and face the coming year with such excitement, knowing that God is leading me and guiding me. He is with me and He is in me.

"Thank you, Father, for this life. Use me for your glory."

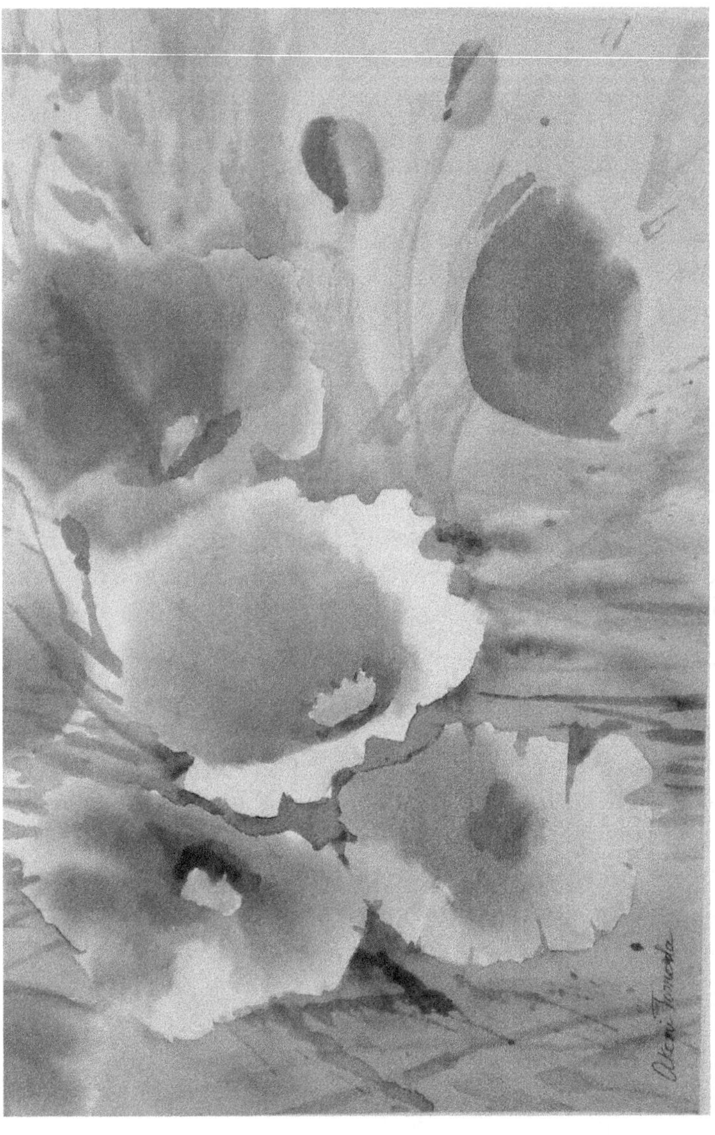

24

The Winter with God's Peace

February 6, 2019

The winter of 2019 is so different. Some days were freezing cold for weeks, and some days were unusually warm. We had lots of snow that melted quickly, and later freezing rain fell.

After a quiet, comfortable December and January, on the 19th of January, we had a huge snowstorm. It started falling around 11:00 o'clock, and it kept on coming all day until the following morning and accumulated more than 30 centimeters of snow.

Around 3:00 o'clock, I wore a special jacket, boots and gloves and cleaned the driveway with my snowblower that Gary gave me years ago. The snowblower is still working, and I enjoy cleaning my driveway and my neighbour Pat's driveway. It was a little cold that day at -17 degrees Celsius during the day. My face was cold, but my heart was rejoicing with thankfulness towards God. The last few years I had so much pain in my right shoulder and in my knees, so that cleaning snow wasn't an easy thing to do, but this winter I was able to use the snowblower again. The snowblower worked very well, and I was so happy to clean the driveway. When I finished the clearing, I removed any snow from the snowblower and put it into the garage, and I truly thanked God. I realized that I had such peace and contentment from God.

Snow kept on coming. Around 7:00 o'clock at night, I thought I had to clean the driveway again, and I opened the entrance door and checked the outside, and found that Pat had cleared my driveway too so I did not do it that night. The next morning on the 20th of January, I cleaned mine and Pat's driveway again before I went to church. Again, I thanked God that I was able to do it this winter, and I truly enjoyed pushing the snowblower. It works so beautifully. After this long cold weather, suddenly we had unusually warm weather on the 3rd and 4th of February. It was so warm that the snow started melting. I did not have to wear a heavy jacket. It was very comfortable.

On the 3rd of February, when I came home from church, I wanted to do grocery shopping, because it had been too cold to go out for many days. I have never done grocery shopping on a Sunday, but I decided to go to Metro. I ate lunch quickly and checked the bus schedule and took my buggy and took a bus and went to Meadowvale Town Centre. At Metro, I picked up some groceries and came home by bus. I enjoyed shopping on such a warm day and thanked God for that.

The following morning on the 4th of February, while I was eating breakfast a thought came to me that it would be nice to visit my family doctor and renew my prescription, so I took a bus again and went to the Meadowvale Town Centre again. I thought I would have to wait a long time, but when I went to the doctor's office I did not have to wait for a long time. Dr. Sarangiwalla gave me a prescription very soon, and I went to Shoppers Drug Mart and I got pills and came home in the bus comfortably. I was so glad that I did it on such a warm day. The temperature went up to 12 degrees Celsius in the middle of the winter and the streets were clean. I thanked God again and again on the bus. I realized that I had such peace from God, that was so precious.

When I arrived at home, I wanted to thank God officially. After I put away the medicines, I sat on the sofa in the living room and started thanking God. "Father, thank you, I was able to see the doctor so easily, and got the pills, I thank you. I never thought of seeing my doctor today, and also yesterday. I never thought of shopping, but I was able to do that. Father, thank you I do everything with your peace. I am so content with who I am and what I do. You are my Father, and I am your daughter, and I am so thankful for that."

While I was thanking God, suddenly I remembered the word God gave to me about 18 years ago. I remember the winter of 2001. I had a very hard time to go through that winter after my husband's death. I said to God, "Father, could you take me home soon? It's very hard to go through the winter by myself. I don't want to go through many winters." Then he said to me, "Akemi, my daughter, you haven't found out how good I am and will be in your life yet."

I remembered our conversation so clearly and thought that God was telling me about the peace of God. If I live my life with His peace no matter what happened. that is the goodness of God in my life. I sensed that He wanted to give me His peace, and He wanted me to experience it in my life.

"My peace I give you. I do not give to you as the world gives. Do not let your heart be troubled and do not be afraid." ~ John 14:27

This peace God wanted to give me, I really thanked God for this life. I can live my life with God and with His peace. What kind of life is it? I realized that God wants me to experience so many of His blessings.

I truly thanked God for His peace and looked back on my life. Since I asked him to "take me home," 18 winters have passed. He has protected me and provided for me so wonderfully and has sent so many people to help me in so many ways. I am experiencing the 19th winter with such peace and contentment. I'm very thankful for that. I don't know how many more winters I will go through, but I know for certain that I will enjoy many winters with His peace, and His joy, and I will find more and more of His goodness in my life. What an exciting life is it!

In the middle of the winter of the year 2019, I had a beautiful time with God and I remember the word God gave to me recently.

"Now may the Lord of peace himself give you peace at all times and in every way. The Lord be with you." ~ 2 Thessalonians 3:16

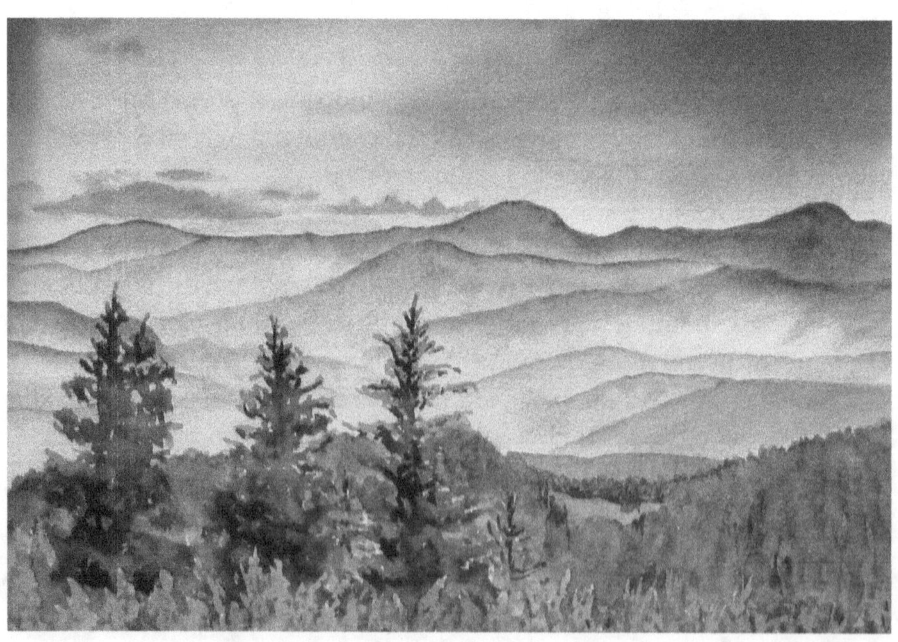

25

I Will See You Again

March 16, 2019

Early in the morning of the 5th of March, while I was still in bed, the telephone rang. When I answered a man said, "Hi Akemi, this is Gordon Fukushima."

"Yes," I answered.

"Akemi, your sister-in-law Yaye passed away last night," he said.

"Thank you for telling me. Was it a peaceful ending?" I asked.

"Yes, it was. She passed away very peacefully," he replied.

I was pleased to hear that. I got out of the bed and thank God. God had waited for her to receive Jesus for 100 years and when she received Jesus as her Savior and Lord, he took her home very quickly. It was truly awesome. I thanked God for giving me courage to tell her about Jesus only three months before.

I met Yaye in the year 1970, when I married Ken at Toronto City Hall. Yaye visited us from Thunder Bay and attended our wedding and celebrated our marriage. Since then, Ken and I visited her in Thunder Bay several times and also she visited us a few times, but I never told her about Jesus. I did not have the courage to introduce Jesus to her even though I was praying for her salvation every morning.

When my husband passed away suddenly from a massive heart attack, Yaye visited me and attended Ken's memorial service. At that time, she found out for the first time that Ken had become a Christian and died as a Christian. She was truly surprised with the beautiful service and that many people gathered to celebrate Ken's going to heaven. She was with me for a few days and left. I could not introduce Jesus to her then.

After 11 years, I published my book Akemi's Journal unexpectedly.

In that book, I wrote nothing but God's blessings in my life and wanted to share it with Yaye, but I could not do it for a long time. After half a year, I decided to send my book to Yaye and called her and said, "I published my book. May I send one to you? I wrote about you in my book."

Then she said, "You wrote about me without asking permission?"

I was really shocked, but I said "I will send one to you. Please read it."

I wrote about Yaye's dream about Ken after his death. She told me that she had a dream about Ken. In her dream Yaye went to say goodbye to Ken in a coffin, but he wasn't there. He was sitting outside the coffin. When Yaye said to Ken, "You are supposed to be dead," Ken said, "I am not dead. I am alive." Yaye also told me that he looked so young with black hair.

That dream confirmed to me that Ken is alive in heaven.

That's all I wrote about Yaye.

I sent my book to Yaye, but I did not hear from her for more than two months. I did not know how to think, I just kept on praying for her salvation.

After a long two months, she finally called me. When I answered her call she said, "I read your book. Thank you for being Ken's wife."

I was so relieved and happy, and I really thanked God for that.

Since Ken's death, we never visited each other, but we talked on the phone often.

Meanwhile Yaye lost her husband too and lived by herself. At that time, she found a good trustee, Mr Gordon Fukushima, and he and his wife looked after her so well.

Yaye started falling often and she was moved to a senior's home and soon a nursing home.

In the year 2016, when I called her at the senior's home, we had a good conversation encouraging each other. Then Yaye said to me suddenly:

"I thank God every morning and every night."

I screamed in my heart "Thank you, Lord. Yaye knows you, and is thanking you!" I thought my job was done.

Soon Yaye was moved to a nursing home. Her trustee Mr Gordon Fukushima looked after her so well. He often called me and told me how Yaye was doing. I really thanked him and also God.

Last July in the year 2018, Yaye celebrated her hundred-year birthday. When I called her and said "Congratulations." She wasn't happy.

She said, "I am very tired and very forgetful." But she spoke perfect Japanese and also perfect English, and her mind was clear.

Then last October, when I talked to her she said, "I don't want to stay here too long. I asked Ken to come and take me with him, but he did not come."

When I heard that, I thought that God can't take her yet. She had to receive Jesus as his Savior and Lord officially. When my prayer partner, Rita, visited me I told her about this situation. Then Rita said, "Let's pray."

She prayed for Yaye's salvation, and her clear mind to receive Jesus, and also prayed for me to have courage to introduce Jesus to her officially.

The following week, I called Yaye and told her that heaven and hell. She agreed to receive Jesus and we prayed the Sinner's Prayer together. Yaye repeated every word I prayed from the beginning to the end. When we said "Amen" Yaye said, "Thank you. You are so kind to me."

One month later, I called her, and she found out she was very tired but peaceful, and another month later Mr. Gordon Fukushima called me and told me that she stopped eating completely, and was sleeping all the time. I just knew it was her time to go home.

When I received a phone call from Mr. Gordon Fukushima and found out that Yaye passed away peacefully, I was so thankful to God. He waited for Yaye to be saved for 100 years, and she is in heaven now. She must have met my husband Ken there too. I look forward to seeing both of them in heaven.

26

I Prayed on My Knees

April 20, 2019

One day in the middle of April, I was painting a birthday card in my workroom. The cold winter was almost gone, and my tax return was taken care of nicely by a professional lady. I was very relaxed and enjoying painting. Then suddenly a memory came back to my mind so clearly. The memory was of when I was kneeling on the workroom wooden floor.

I wondered why I was remembering that, but I remembered it continually. It was about 30 years ago in the middle of April. I was on the floor and asking God for money. That year my husband Ken had a nervous breakdown and could not go to work for about seven months. Because he could not go to work, his salary was reduced quite a lot, and in the middle of April, I found that we did not have enough money for the next month's mortgage. I remember so clearly how I felt and how worried I was for money, and also for Ken's health. His doctor said that some people takes six to seven months to recover, but some people take two to three years.

I even remembered how I prayed to God. I was on the floor facing the blank wall, looking up at the wall and I said:

"Father, as you know we don't have enough money for the next month's mortgage. If you want us to go back to an apartment, we are happy to go back, but if you allow us to stay in this home, we need $500 by the 1st of May. Would you take care of this? I ask in Jesus's name. Amen."

I remembered when I finished my prayer and got up from the floor, a thought came to me that we could ask for money from my sister-in-law in Thunder Bay. When that thought came to me, I said,

"Thank you, Father, now I know that we can borrow money from my sister-in-law. I never thought of that before. Thank you."

I asked my husband to call Yaye and he did. Yaye sent us a cheque very quickly and I forgot about this problem completely.

When May 1st came, Ken received a letter from the government as a tax return, and he received $1900 back. I remember that I was on the wooden floor in my workroom again and asked God for forgiveness. I said, "Father, forgive me. I did not trust you. I asked you for $500 by the 1st of May, and soon we got money from Yaye. I am so sorry. Please forgive me. You gave us $1900 on the day exactly as I asked. I really like to trust you. Help me to trust you completely. I can return money to Yaye soon. You are my wonderful provider. I feel so safe to live my life with your help. Thank you."

I remembered all these things so clearly. I sensed it was not just my memory, but it's from God. He reminded me of this event.

I went to the bookshelf in the closet and found the budget book of 1985. When I opened the page of April, I found that Ken was out of work the whole month, and on the page of May be received 1,925 dollars from the government on the 1st of May. I also found that Ken returned to work on the 14th of June, after six months of sick leave.

It was exactly 34 years ago, the memory came back to me so clearly and I thought that since then I have never asked God for money, not even a penny. He had met all our needs, and after my husband's death, He met all my needs.

I stopped painting and sat on the wooden floor again, but this time I could not sit nicely because of my knee. But I was on the floor again and praying to God exactly like I did 34 years ago. I prayed, "Father, thank you. You meet all my needs. I asked you to meet our needs 34 years ago. Since then I have never asked you for more money anymore. You are my good provider and faithful provider. I feel so secure knowing that my God meets all my needs. Thank you very much. You are a wonderful Father!"

When I finished my prayer, I felt so awesome to have lived my life with God's help. I completed my painting with lots of thanksgiving in my heart to God.

It was so unusual to remember what I did 34 years ago so clearly. I believe that God wanted me to know His promises, that He is with me. Even though I went through a very hard time, He was with me and listening to my prayers and answered my prayers. He never left me or forsook of me.

I sensed that God was speaking to me, "Akemi, my daughter, I'm with you all the time. When you go through a good time, I am with you, and when you go through a very difficult time, I am with you. Don't look at problems, but look at me and receive my peace, my joy from me. I am always with you and will go with you. Look at me and trust me. I will go with you. I want you to enjoy our journey together."

I truly thanked God for this beautiful life with God.

April of 2019 is going very quickly. We had a very cold and long winter, but it's going, and the new spring is coming. Then the new shoots have started coming out in the Lord's garden, and I am so excited to look after His garden again this year. We had lots of rain, and every day the plants are growing strongly. I know that I will have a good spring and summer in His garden and will enjoy His presence very much. I also expect lots of wonderful surprises from God.

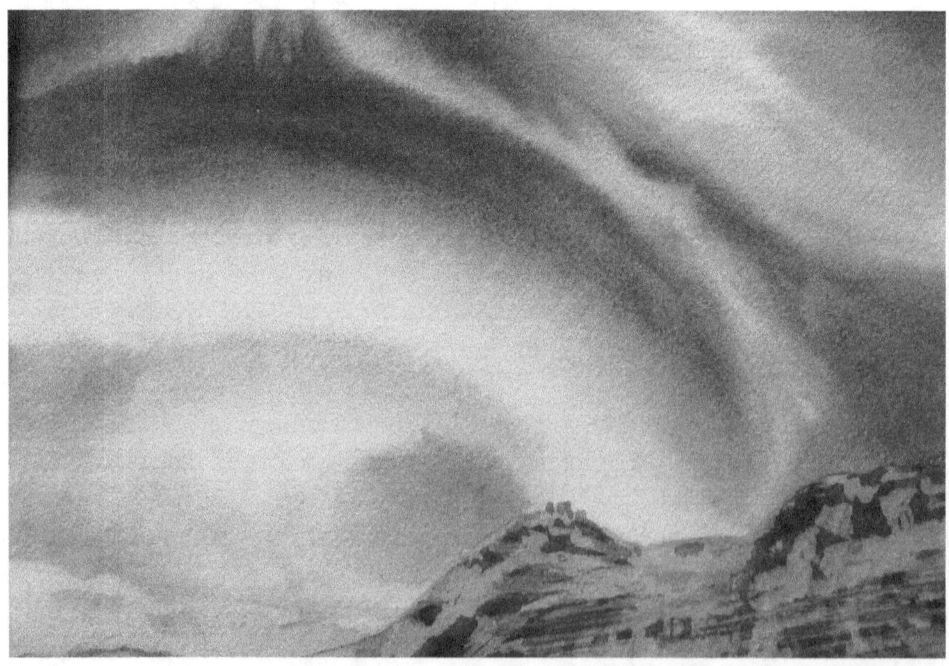

27

The Precious Gathering

May 12, 2019

In the year 2000, right after my husband's death, Rita took me to her home group of Toronto Airport Church. I wasn't a member of that church, but everyone welcomed me. Rita drove me to Bill and Sue Dupley's house and drove me home. Bill and Sue were the leaders. They were spirit filled and anointed wonderful leaders who were on fire for the Lord. I learned so much. I felt so comfortable being there. I also came to know many friends there.

One day, Heather, one of the ladies from the group approached me and asked me if we could get together occasionally, so I said, "Yes."

Then soon Heather Casuel, Janice Orr, Rita Gervais and I decided to get together for lunch once a month. One lady prepared the meat, one lady the veggies, one lady the salad, and one lady the dessert.

I believe it was 15 or 16 years ago that we first met. We met together and ate a delicious lunch and spent time together. It was a very relaxing and comfortable gathering together, and I enjoyed it very much. We get together faithfully once a month and enjoyed each other's fellowship.

I found out that my three friends are such good cooks. They cooked very delicious food every time we met. When I could not eat so many things because of my sensitive nervous system, they called me to check with me and if I could not eat then they cooked my portion separately. I was truly overwhelmed by their kindness.

They came to my home, because I live alone, and nobody bothers us. We got together so faithfully and enjoyed such good food and each other's fellowship for many years.

While we were meeting together once a month, the meeting

changed direction from just a comfortable meeting to growing spiritually. We started praying for each other. I'm so excited to have three wonderful sisters in my home once a month, each one of us went through many difficult times, but we never stopped meeting together. We also celebrated our birthdays with delicious food and a birthday cake and birthday gifts, Heather in March, Rita in May, Akemi in October and Janice in December. When I became 80, they celebrated my 80th birthday with more friends and a wonderful lunch and prayers. I was so touched by the kindness.

We have been doing this for at least 15 years, but we never get tired of it. I truly love my friends. These ladies are so committed to God and love God so much! They are also so deep in His word, and Bible verses come out in their conversation so freely. I am so thankful that God put us together and blesses us. I sensed that God is smiling on us.

This month we got together on the 9th of May. It was Rita's birthday. In the morning, I prepared the table for our lunch as usual, knives and forks, napkins, plates, glasses. When I finished my preparation, I prayed a short prayer as usual. "Lord, the ladies are coming here today. Bless us. Your will be done. May your purpose for the gathering be fulfilled."

Rita came at 11:45 and we chatted a little while watching my backyard where the perennials had started growing suddenly after a long and cold winter. Janice and Heather came a little after 12 with food and birthday gifts. We greeted each other. They know my house and kitchen so well that they were able to do everything in the kitchen, warming up the meat in the oven and putting things in my fridge.

When the food was on the table, we sat on the chairs and held hands together and prayed to God and gave thanks to God. Then we ate some delicious chicken drumsticks which Janice cooked, and roasted vegetables which Rita prepared, and salad which I prepared. We really enjoyed the delicious food and conversation. I felt so relaxed and comfortable to be with my friends.

After the meal, we celebrated Rita's birthday with a birthday cake which Heather had baked along with candles and cups of tea or coffee. We sang "Happy birthday to you" for Rita and took photos and enjoyed eating the delicious cake.

When we finished eating the cake, we washed the dishes very quickly and sat on the sofas. We took up birthday gifts to Rita, and Rita opened the gifts one by one. After opening the gifts and cards, we prayed over Rita for God's continual blessings over her and her beautiful future with God. Then suddenly God joined us.

Rita started saying, "I see the glory of God. It's so beautiful! It's so awesome!"

We all stood up and glorified God. It was truly an awesome moment. God touched each one of us. We read Bible verses and prayed for each other confirming His great love and blessings on us to continue in living wonderful lives with the Lord.

The time went so fast and we quickly decided on the date for our next gathering. Janice and Heather left at 4:00 o'clock. We had a truly beautiful time with each other and God, and I truly thanked him for that.

As I cleaned the table and the kitchen, Rita was with me in the kitchen and said, "Akemi, the glory of God is here in the kitchen!" She screamed and fell on the kitchen floor. It was truly awesome! I thanked God for His presence. Rita and I spent more time in the kitchen and enjoyed the presence of God immensely.

Then Rita said, "Akemi, you are a wonderful gift from God."

I said, "Thank you, Rita. You are a wonderful gift for me."

We hugged each other in my kitchen.

Rita left with her birthday gifts. It started raining as I watched Rita's car move away in the rain.

I truly thanked God for the wonderful gathering we had. Our gathering has become more and more spiritual each time. Our precious journey towards God's heart continues. I am so excited for the next gathering in June when we meet at Janice's house. I asked Father to bless us again in our next gathering.

28

Bill Dupley's 65th B'day Party

June 25, 2019

One day in early June, Sue Dupley called me and said, "Akemi, I would like to invite you to Bill's 65th birthday celebration on the 23rd of June. I want you to come."

"Thank you very much. If Rita goes, I will go with her," I said.

"Vi is coming and Janice is coming. Please join us," Sue said. I really thanked her for her kind invitation.

Later when I talked to Rita, I asked her if she could attend Bill's birthday party. Then Rita said, "You know that Sunday afternoon I have a meeting with the French group. I don't think I can go." So, I decided not to attend Bill's birthday party.

After that, I thought about Bill and Sue's home group meeting a lot. Right after my husband's death, Rita took me to her home group meeting at Bill and Sue Dupley's home in Meadowvale, and I met them for the first time. There were many people from the Toronto Airport Church, and they took me into the family. I had a great time there. Bill and Sue helped me to go through a very hard time in my life. They prayed over me often and encouraged me. Sue took me too Sumie's art class one day, and she took me to her friend's garage sale where she was selling lots of fabric at very inexpensive prices and I bought a lot of fabric there. When I looked back, I realized that I had met many Christians through Bill and Sue, and I really thanked God for that.

After a couple of weeks, when I met Rita, she said that the 23rd afternoon's meeting had been cancelled, so that we were able to attend Bill's birthday party and be prepared a plate to take.

We had so many rainy days this spring, but on the 23rd, it was a beautiful sunny day. Rita took me to her church, Catch the Fire Toronto, and we attended the Sunday service there. I listened to a good teaching about the Holy Spirit and was very satisfied. After this service, we went to Tim Horton's and ate a quick lunch and went to Rita's place and picked up her plate and came back to my house to pick up a plate and two folding chairs. Then we drove to Carlisle in Hamilton where they moved years ago. When we arrived at the Dupley's place, it was already 3:30 PM.

The street in front of the Dupley's house was packed with many cars, and also on their driveway. Bill and Sue have a beautiful house with a large backyard with a pool and a vegetable garden and also a flower garden. They both are retired and are enjoying their lives.

When we walked through their house and got into the backyard, two tents were set up, and many people were sitting on their folding chairs. I did not know the majority of the people there.

Bill came to us and greeted us warmly. "Akemi, thank you for coming," he said with a big hug, and showed me his vegetable garden where vegetables were growing healthily in a tiny spot next to their home. He said, "This is my gift for Sue. This is her art house where she can do stained glass and ceramics." He also introduced me to his neighbours.

We joined the group and talked and ate appetizers in the shade of the tree. I met several people from our home group and enjoyed talking to them.

Bill thanked each one of us and invited us for a hamburger and hotdog and lots of salads. We ate and talked in a beautiful funny garden.

While I was in the garden and surrounded by old friends from the home group many years ago, I remembered the time I spent in Bill and Sue's house. At that time, Bill was teaching us seriously about "hearing from God." He gave each of us a piece of paper and a pencil and invited us to imagine that we were with Jesus. He said, "Close your eyes and imagine where you are with Jesus. It could be on a lake shore or in the garden, wherever you like. Every time he said that I imagined I was with Jesus in my backyard, sitting on the garden chairs and drinking a cup of tea or walking in the garden holding hands tightly.

Bill asked a question to God and then said to us, "Now you write down what God is saying to you." The first time I heard this, I was so shocked and doubted if I could hear from God or not. But everybody started writing on their papers. The room was so quiet and only slight pencil sounds were there.

I was in trouble and said to God in my heart, "Lord, speak to me," and I waited. Surprisingly, a thought came to my mind, so I wrote it down. When I finished waiting another thought came to me, so I kept on writing, and I was so thrilled.

After that Bill asked everyone to read what we had written. It was wonderful to hear what God was speaking to His own children in so many different ways. I enjoyed it so much and started listening to God and writing it. That was the most precious gift Bill gave to me, "Hearing from God."

I still do this time to time, open a writing pad, holding a pencil and ask a question to God, and write down whatever comes to my mind. I spent a precious time with God and I enjoyed it very much.

While we were eating and talking, Bill came, so I told him what I had learned from his home group, "Hearing from God" and thanked him. I said, "I still do it sometimes and write it down in my special notebook."

Then Bill said, "That's good! Keep on doing that. That's very important."

People started going home with their own folding chairs and plates. We helped in clearing up the table and plates. Rita drove me home, and when we arrived it was already 8:00 o'clock.

I had a blessed time at Bill and Sue's backyard party and I truly thanked God that I had met Bill and Sue on my life journey, and they helped me in so many ways to continue my journey.

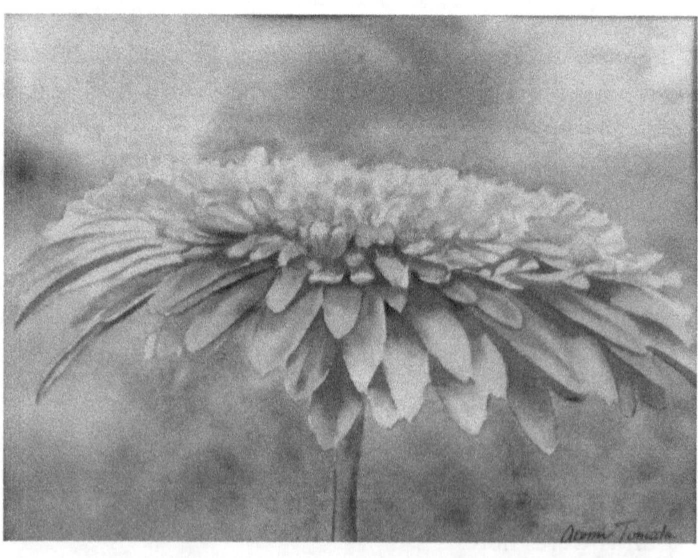

29

Keep on Telling Your Story

July 7, 2019

About a month ago, I had a strange dream. In the dream, I was in a big church, and standing in line waiting for a man to come and talk to me. I did not know who he was, but he was coming closer to me very slowly. He was blessing everyone in the line, holding hands or touching them one by one giving them words of encouragement.

When he came a little closer to me, I saw his face and realized that I had met him before. I could not remember where or when, but definitely I knew him, and I wanted to talk to him so badly. My heart started beating fast and I said in my mind, "Please come to me and talk to me."

Eventually the man came very close to me. He touched the person standing next to me and blessed her. He came to me and stood in front of me. I was so happy and looked at his eyes, and I knew that I had met him before. He took my hands with both his hands and looked at me. His eyes were so beautiful and gentle, I was in awe. Then he said to me, "Keep on telling your stories."

"Yes, I will," I said.

Then suddenly I woke up from my sleep.

Did I talk to Jesus? I wondered for awhile. I really did not know who he was, but I just knew that God sent that man to talk to me. I was so encouraged by the dream and was determined to write about "The Goodness of God in my Life." If anyone should read my essays and be encouraged by them, I am very happy, and God is pleased.

On the 4th of July, I attended a church, Life House Church, prayer meeting at the church office. My friend Anne Hanson gave me a ride and we went to the room where we meet. Anne went out of the room, so I was alone in the room. I thanked God that I was able to attend the prayer meeting, and also prayed that His will be done in our meeting. While I was praying, Leigh Colgan, a pastor's wife came into the room with a big smile, and said, "Good morning, Akemi."

"Good morning. How are you?" I said.

She gave me a big hug and said, "Are you coming for the ladies breakfast tomorrow?"

"No, I am not," I said.

"Can you come as my guest?"

"What time is it?" I asked.

"From 9 to 11."

I thought about it. If it finishes at 11, I can still do my housework on Saturday, so I said, "Yes, I can make it. How much is it?"

"$10."

"Then I will pay now."

"No, no. I want you to be my guest. I am glad you can come. By the way, can you give us a testimony?"

"What?"

"Just a short testimony, about five minutes. Fifty ladies are coming," she said.

"Oh," I replied.

"Akemi, I am so glad you can come. I will see you on Saturday."

"Leigh, I need a ride. I don't drive a car anymore."

At that moment, Anne came back into the room, so Leigh said to Anne, "Anne, could you give Akemi a ride on Saturday?"

"Yes, I can," Anne said.

"That settled," Leigh said and left the room. I was surprised at what just happened. I looked back on my life, and I realized that the Lord has given me several opportunities to speak of His goodness in front of people at church, at a book launch. It is so strange that I am speaking of "The Goodness of God" in front of people in English. I said in my heart, "Lord, you are amazing. You want me to tell people about your goodness in English?" I smiled to myself.

Our meeting lasted longer than three hours. Soon Anne drove me home. After I eat a simple lunch, I started preparing my testimony with a pencil and writing pad. Then I remembered that my testimony was in a book called, "Then and Now," published by In Our Words Inc, this spring. The publisher, Cheryl Antao-Xavier included my essay in it.

I took out the book "Then and Now" and read my essay and

thought that was perfect for the Saturday's ladies breakfast gathering. I felt so at ease because my friends and I were visiting our old friend Adele in a nursing home in Port Dover on Friday. I would take a whole day to prepare another testimony. I thanked God that I have something to share with the ladies.

On Friday, Rita picked up Dianne and me and we went to see Adele. It was a very hot and humid day, but we had a good time, and we prayed for each other, and ate a delicious lunch. We arrived home at 4:30, and then I attended our home group from 7 to 10. I was so relieved that I did not have to prepare my speech.

On Saturday the 5th of July, Anne gave me a ride and we went to our new church office. On the 2nd floor, there were already many ladies, and tables and chairs were arranged very nicely. We had a very delicious breakfast with worship, and four ladies each gave a testimony. I was asked to speak first. I told everybody that I was going to read my essay from a book and I read it. It took about five minutes.

I read how I became a Christian, and I met Ken in Japan, and came to Canada, and was married to Ken. After many long years of prayer, Ken became a Christian. We had good times together, reading the Bible together and praying together, and then Ken's sudden death. I went through the darkest time in my life. I cried out to God for His help. How God helps me and healed me by sending kind people into my life and also through writing essays about "The Goodness of God in my Life," painting watercolour paintings and looking after the garden. I told them that one day God spoke to me, "Thank you for looking after my garden." That made me so happy, and I enjoyed spending time with God in the garden.

When I finished reading my essay, the ladies gave me a big applause. I enjoyed the rest of the meeting, listening to three other ladies giving their testimonies. I had a very nice time at the ladies' breakfast, and Anne drove me home. When I came home, I felt so peaceful and thanked God for what I was able to do.

That night while I was lying in bed, suddenly I remembered the dream I had a month ago. A man with beautiful eyes came to me and took my hands and said, "Keep on telling your stories."

I thanked God that He provided a place to share my story. I said, "Father, thank you for today. I was able to tell the ladies of your goodness. I'm so happy and blessed! I am yours. Use me for your glory." Then I slept.

30

Finding Treasures

July 19, 2019

We had a steady rain the whole of last night, and when I woke up at 6:30 on the 18th of July, I still heard the sound of rain. I was so glad because the land was so dry with the hot weather and the plants needed a steady rain.

In the morning, I decided to clean up my unfinished artwork. When I paint with watercolours, sometimes it does not turn out the way I hope, and I just keep the unfinished paintings in a special drawer. Recently I started fixing them, and I enjoyed it.

This morning I fixed two landscape paintings. I added a little yellow on the dark green leaves, and made the tree trunks darker, and added more branches. I enjoyed fixing the unfinished paintings.

When I finished, I checked the drawer above where I kept many printed papers from the art classes I attended. While I was checking the drawer, my fingers touched some very hard papers. I did not know what they were. I pulled them out and found seven of my mother's artwork. She tore coloured papers and glued them on a hard paper and made beautiful artwork, small chrysanthemums, trees, fruits, shrimp, etc. They were so beautiful and elegant. I was stunned.

I put them on the table and looked at them. I did not remember when my sister had sent them to me, probably right after my mother's death, but I was so happy as if I was talking to my mother. I looked at her work for a long time and thanked God for my mother. She started doing artwork after my father passed away. She was already over 70 years old, but she enjoyed it. I was so thankful for that. My mother had a good time. I received a gift of creativity through my mother. Now I am enjoying immensely painting watercolours, gardening, and sewing, which makes my life so happy.

I tried to display my mother's artwork, but I did not have a big enough frame, so I decided to do it some other day, but I was so happy as if I had found a treasure.

When I came down to the kitchen to make my lunch, I stood behind the kitchen counter, and looked outside. I saw a small green garden table and two chairs on the deck in the rain, and I saw a big white bag on the garden table and wondered what it was. I watched carefully one more time and decided to go out in the rain. When I went out and checked the white bag, it was a plastic grocery bag and had groceries in it. I picked up the wet plastic bag and came back into the kitchen. The bag was labeled Metro and there were two mangoes, two lemons, a few bananas, grapes and one broccoli. I took out all the groceries and put them on the counter wondering who brought this gift for me.

A few of my friends' names came to my mind, but I did not know who sent this gift. How could I find the sender of the gift? I wondered. I thanked God in my heart that he surrounded me with kind people, and I was so blessed. While I was putting the fruit in the fridge, I saw Jim, who lives in front of my house sitting on a chair in his garage listening to his radio as he often does. I decided to visit him and ask him if he saw someone come to my house this morning.

When I opened the entrance door, Jim saw me, so I waved my hand wide and he responded to me. I got out of the house and started running towards him, and he came out of the garage. I said, "How are you, Jim? Are you alright?"

"Yes, I am very much better now," he said. Jim had tongue cancer and received treatment. I was glad that he looked better now.

I said, "I would like to ask you Jim, did you see anybody come to my house this morning?"

Then Jim said, "Yes, I saw a lady going to your house."

"Who was she?" I asked.

"The lady from over there." He pointed to a house beside us.

"Oh Marianne?"

"Yes, that's her. She went to your house about 30 minutes ago."

"Thank you." I told Jim that I had received a grocery bag on the garden table. I walked to Marianne's house and rang the doorbell. After a little while, Marianne's husband opened the door.

"Hi, I came to say thank you to Marianne. She left a grocery bag on my garden table."

"Oh really? She is out now."

"Please say thank you to her. I really appreciate her kindness."

"Yes, I will tell her. I did not know what she did."

"Thank you. Bye." I came home. The rain stopped completely. I thanked God again for the kind people he has sent me in my life.

Marianne lives a few houses down from me. We have lived on the street many years, but we never talked before. Only last year, Judas, a lady who lives on our street introduced me saying, "Akemi, Marianne lives over there. She is an artist too. You should meet her." So, one day while she was at the front of her house, I visited her. I introduced myself and told her that I loved art. Then she took me into her house and showed me her paintings, which were on the walls of her house. They were beautiful paintings. She also told me that she doesn't paint anymore.

After I saw Marianne's artwork, I invited her to my house and showed her my husband's and my paintings all over my house. We did not see each other often, but we became good friends.

I learned that Marianne stopped attending church after her son's death, but her husband goes to church every Sunday. Her son was married to an evangelist. I was so glad that I met a Jesus believer on a street and hoped that someday we could pray together for the Salvation of the people who live on our street.

In the afternoon, I took out of one of my books Akemi's Journals II and signed it and took it to Marianne. I visited her house again. This time Marianne opened the door.

I said, "Marianne, thank you so much for your kind gift this morning. You are so kind. This is my gift for you." I presented my book to her.

Then she said, "You don't have to return anything to me," and she checked the book and said, "Oh it's your book, is it?"

"Yes, these are my essays, and my paintings are in it too."

"Thank you very much. Did you write about God?"

"Yes, the goodness of God in my life."

"I appreciate it. Thank you."

She invited me into her living room. We sat on the sofa and had a cold drink, which she had made. I had a very comfortable time with Marianne and came home with a big thanksgiving in my heart.

I had a precious day on the 18th of July, enjoying my mother's artwork and a heartfelt kind gift from Marianne.

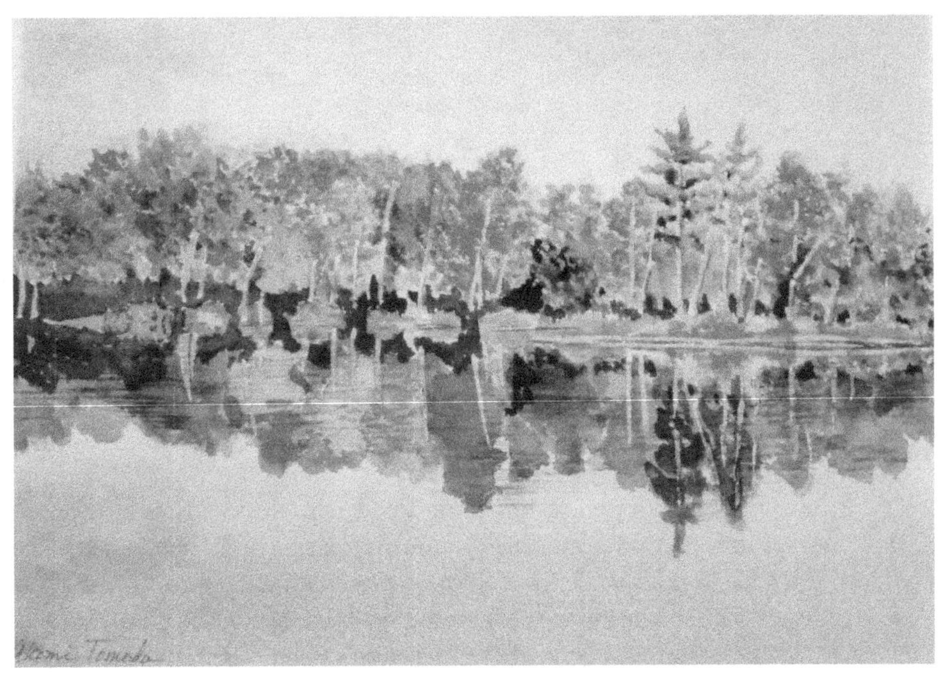

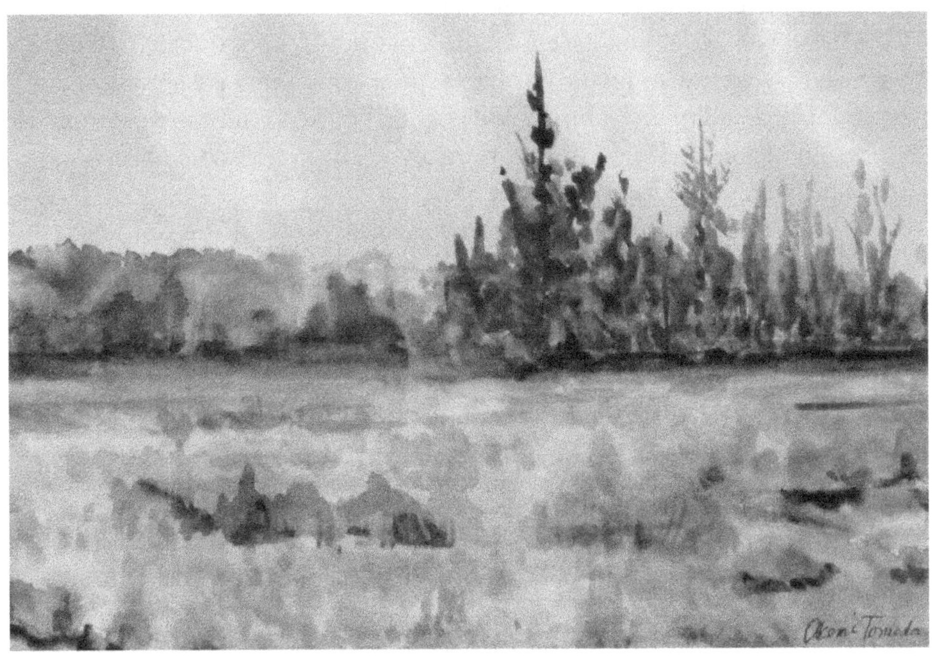

31

"What are You Saying to Me?"

August 1, 2019

Since the snow stopped, it has rained and rained the whole spring. We had lots of rain continually until the end of June. I never watered the garden until the end of June. It has been a very cool spring, but because of all the rain, the perennials grew so tall and bushy. I never saw the perennials grow that much. In the early spring, the tulips grew so high and bloomed huge flowers. Everything grew so high, and the spring flowers lasted so long.

Every time I looked at the garden, I asked the Lord, "Lord, what are you saying to me through this garden?"

God is pouring out an enormous amount of rain, double portion of rain on the earth. I truly believe that the same thing is happening in the spiritual realm too. The double portion of God's anointing, double portion of His presence, double portion of His fire, double portion of His healing are pouring out from Him.

I just pray that God will touch everyone who visits the Lord's garden deeply.

The perennials grew and grew. They formed double portions of buds. It was truly awesome. I truly enjoyed watching them. Every morning was different from the previous day.

One morning, I found five extra large leaves on the vine covering the "Gate to Heaven." These leaves were 10 times larger than other leaves and facing towards the living room. When I saw them I was stunned. I could not move my eyes from them. Gazing at the five huge leaves I said to God, "Lord, what are you saying to me through these large leaves?"

Is God saying to me that this year is different from other years, or is he telling me there is a great harvest in the year. I pondered about it. I really did not know what He was saying to me, but I truly thanked God that I am living my life in this exciting time.

When we had our Bible study, I asked my friends about the extraordinary bushy garden. Then Rita and Ellie, who both attended the Catch the Fire Toronto spring conference, said that many speakers said that this year is a year of great harvest, and lots of people will come to know the Lord.

I was so happy to know that many people are sensing the same thing from God. I prayed to God that a great harvest will come to Japan too. It would be so wonderful if the Japanese people are set free completely from the enemies' plan and start worshipping the only true God.

By watching the healthy growing garden, I also sensed that God is saying to me, "Grow healthy in my garden, grow strongly in my garden. I want you to bloom beautifully. I enjoy watching you."

I was so encouraged and thought that there is no limit in growing in the Lord's garden.

Because of the unusually cold spring in May and June, the perennials did not bloom in June. I had to wait until July. Flowers did not bloom in the springtime, but I realized there were unusually many buds on every perennial. More than double portion of buds were growing on every plant. At the beginning of July, the flowers started opening little by little. Shasta daisy started opening, and yarrow followed, and meadowsweet started opening one by one, and Akinesia opened slowly. I enjoyed watching every day and was amazed by so many flowers opening. Every plant opened with more than double the flowers than the other years.

My garden was covered with many different coloured flowers. I was in awe. I had never seen such a beautiful garden before. Since my husband Ken moved to heaven in the year 2000, I have looked after the garden for 19 years, but I have never seen so many flowers like this year. It is like an explosion of flowers. On top of that, many birds and butterflies were flying over the flowers. I never got tired of looking at the garden, saying in my heart, "Lord, what are you saying to me with this garden? If you are saying to me that your love is beautiful and huge like this garden or your plans and dreams for my life is beautiful like this?"

Looking at the explosion of flowers, I thanked God for giving me this experience to taste His power and beauty. I said in my heart many times, "Lord, use this garden for your glory. Use me for your glory." I invited many of my neighbours and my friends into the garden.

One day I saw Jim, who lives in front of my house, sitting in his garage, and listening to the radio. Jim had tongue cancer and has completed treatment. I decided to invite him into the Lord's garden. I crossed the street and walked to him, and said, "Jim, I would like to invite you to my garden. Would you like to see it?"

"Of course," he said.

We walked together to cross the street again.

"You have never seen my backyard, have you?"

"No, I haven't," he said.

"Good, you know this year is a special year. So many flowers are blooming." We walked through the garage and went to the backyard.

"Wow! Look at this! It's so beautiful!" Jim was stunned.

"Isn't it beautiful? That's why I invited you."

"Akemi, thank you. You made my day."

"I'm glad you like it," I said.

I had a good time in the garden. When he was leaving, I said, "I hope you will be healed completely."

"Well, I don't expect too much now," Jim said.

"I'm expecting your complete healing, because I have been praying to God for your healing every morning," I said.

"Thank you, Akemi." Jim gave me a big hug and left.

I invited my neighbours on both sides, Stephanie and her son came and enjoyed my garden, and Pat came and was surprised by so many flowers. I had a good time with my neighbours and thanked God for that and hoped that God touched them by His grace.

Many more of my friends visited the garden and they had a wonderful time surrounded by many beautiful flowers.

I asked God, "Lord, is this a piece of heaven you are showing me? Will I see a more beautiful garden in heaven?"

I truly thanked God for his beautiful creation!

32

At Widad's Hair Salon

September 2, 2019

Since I stopped driving my car, my hairdresser, Widad Samaan, has looked after me so well. Every time I needed a treatment for my hair, she drove to my house and then drove me to her house where she had made a beautiful hair salon in her basement. She looked after my hair and drove me home again.

Since 2017, Widad kept on helping me so kindly. I am so thankful for that. Widad is a professional hair stylist and also a passionate Christian. I learned that her father was a pastor, and that her whole family are devoted to the Lord so faithfully. I feel so peaceful and also so comfortable to be with her in her beautiful salon. I truly thanked God that I met her on my life journey.

Every time I made an appointment, Widad came to my house at 10:00 o'clock, and drove me to her home. Widad has a beautiful hair salon in her basement with a big mirror and a black sink, a table, chest, and the cabinet. It is a very comfortable salon. Every time I was there, there was soft music in the air. Recently when I go there, Widad changes it to the classical music station, which is my favourite station. I am so spoiled!

After she puts colour on my hair, she sets a timer and goes upstairs to her kitchen and prepares a hot drink and brings our drinks with her homemade snacks. We enjoy a teatime in the elegant salon for awhile. I am so thankful for that too.

Her little salon's wall was painted with beige-coloured paint, and a little darker colour for decoration close to the ceiling. The front side wall was occupied by a huge mirror and a sample paper of hair colours. On the right side of the wall, a wall clock is hanging, and a black sink.

On the left side of the wall, a calendar of my garden is hanging. I take photos from my garden every year, and choose 12 pictures from January to December, and take them to The UPS Store. They make beautiful calendars for me every year. Right after my husband moved to heaven, I started making calendars in the memory of my husband. Since then, calendars from my garden became my Christmas gifts for many of my friends who helped me in my life.

The calendar is hanging on the left side of the wall, but the rear wall is totally empty. Every time I was in Widad's hair salon and sitting towards the mirror, I looked at the empty wall, and wanted to hang my watercolor paintings so badly.

In June, when Widad picked me up, I wrapped my watercolour painting of red poppies, and took it with me. When we arrived at Widad's House, I took out my painting and said, "This is for you."

"Oh, thank you Akemi," she said, and looked for a place to hang it at the entrance of the house.

I said, "It's for your basement, Widad. There is an empty wall in your salon, and I want you to hang it there."

We went to the basement, and Widad said, "I will ask my husband to put a nail there."

I held the painting of the red poppies with my hands on the wall and said, "Widad, I'm not giving you this painting, when I come next time, I will take it home, but I will bring a new painting."

"Oh, that would be nice! Thank you," she said.

The next time I visited Widad, I took a yellow sunflower painting with me and exchanged the pictures. Widad said that many of her clients enjoyed my painting, and some of them took a photo of it.

I was so pleased and also so excited to decide which painting I should bring next time. It is a pure joy like I have my own art gallery in Widad's basement. I was so glad I took my watercolour paintings there.

One day in July, we had a Bible study at my home. Elli, our leader, Dianne, and Rita came. Dianne brought a book and said to me, "Akemi, I brought a book for you. I want you to read it."

The book was titled Revealing Heaven written by Kat Kerr. I was so interested in knowing about heaven where my husband moved, so I started reading it that night. I truly enjoyed reading the books so much, that I could not stop reading it, and finished the book very quickly.

The author, Kat Kerr wrote about her experience in heaven. She wrote that God took her to heaven many times and showed her many places in heaven and said to her "Write a book about your experience in heaven." So, she wrote this book. I was so excited to read of experiences in heaven. She wrote that when someone dies, God is already preparing a beautiful and huge mansion for that person in heaven. She also wrote that if someone loves art, God prepares a nice art studio in the mansion and he or she will continue to enjoy painting in heaven.

That was truly an eye-opening truth which I never thought of. She also wrote that there is no money in heaven, so that artists paint beautiful paintings and just give them away. When I read that, I was so excited and thought that I am doing the same thing here on earth already. I am already practicing a life in heaven here. What an exciting thing this is.

I said, "Oh God, thank you for this beautiful life. I enjoy painting and to bring one to Widad's space and to display it, for people to enjoy it. I am so blessed! I am also excited to go home, knowing what a beautiful place heaven is!"

I made my next appointment with Widad for the 10th of September and I am planning to bring a picture of the fall scenery.

I am so thankful for Widad's friendship. I will have a blessed time at her hair salon.

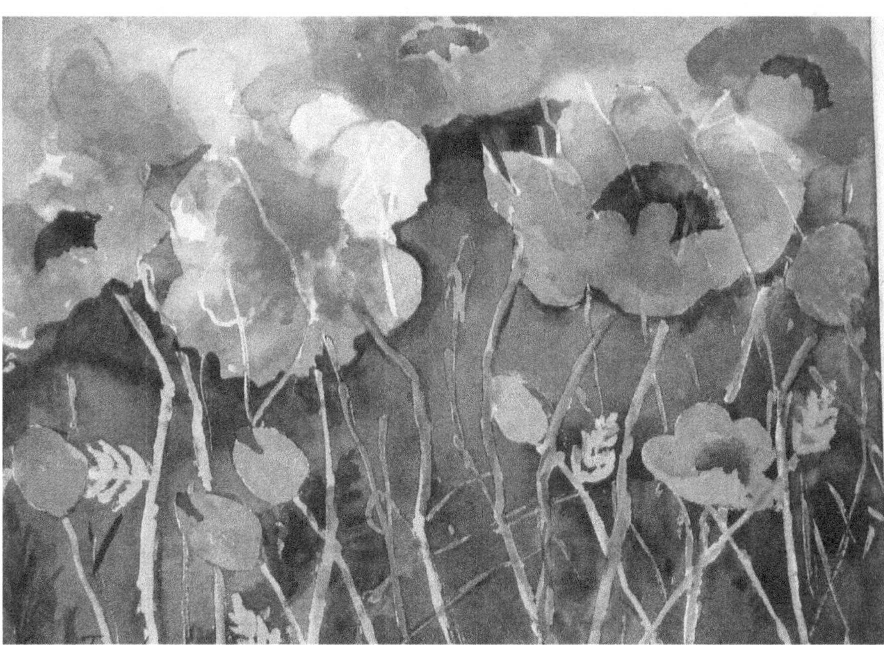

33

Breakfast with Japanese Ladies

September 20, 2019

I attended Yong Wah's prayer meetings with Rita and prayed for Japan seriously for many years. I truly thanked God for the way He is using me.

Yong Wah has run Followers Mission in Toronto for so many years and has invited many people to the Lord. She also visits many countries and teaches God's love passionately.

I truly enjoyed attending the prayer meetings at Yong Wah's house once a month for many years.

But when my nervous system became oversensitive, I had a hard time sitting on a sofa for a long time, so I stopped attending the meeting. I kept on praying for Japan by myself at home. I prayed and prayed for Japan every morning, but I did not know what was happening in Japan at all.

At the end of June, my friend Tatyana told me that Yong Wah was visiting Japan and praying for Japan, and she invited me to attend the next prayer meeting. When I heard that, I just knew that I had to be there, so I asked Rita to take me to the July's prayer meeting.

I was so glad I attended that meeting. I said to Yong Wah, "I came here to say thank you. Thank you very much for visiting Japan and praying for Japan."

At her basement, about a dozen people got together and worshiped God. After the worship, Yong Wah reported about her visit to Japan. Then we all prayed for Japan. I was so glad I attended that night.

While we were praying, a gentleman called Paul had a picture of Japan from the Lord, and he said, "I see a picture of Japanese people who are carrying heavy traditions. I would like to break it from the

Japanese people," and he prayed. I joined his prayer for freedom from deception.

Paul came to me and sat in front of me holding both my legs with his hands and said, "Can I pray for Japan through you?"

"Of course, please pray. Thank you," I said.

He prayed for the Japanese people to receive Jesus as their saviour, and for many people to come to know him. I was so happy to hear that, and also thanked God that I was there on that night.

The next meeting, I could not attend. On the 9th of September, I just knew that I had to be there, so I asked Rita to take me with her.

The evening of the 9th of September, when we arrived at Yong Wah's house, I saw only one car on her driveway. I wondered if the prayer meeting had been cancelled, but the door was open, and we got into the house.

While Rita and I were removing our shoes and wearing slippers, somebody said in the kitchen. "Oh, Rita is here."

Then Yong Wah said, "Oh good. How about Akemi?"

"She is here," someone said.

Soon Yong Wah came out from the kitchen and greeted us. She gave Rita a big hug and said, "Welcome Rita." She also gave me a big hug and said, "Welcome Akemi, I'm so glad you are here tonight."

"Thank you," I said.

Then she said, "You know two ladies are coming from Japan soon, and we will have a breakfast at Akemi's house at 8:30 on the 18th."

"What?" I asked.

I would like to show them how a Japanese lady is living in Canada. We are going to Niagara from your house. We will be at your house at 8:30 and leave at 9:30."

"Wow!" I said. I did not know what to say. I had to prepare breakfast for three ladies at 8:30. I wondered what time I had to wake up or what to cook. Then Rita said immediately, "I will help you Akemi. Don't worry."

"Thank you, Rita, then I can do that."

The prayer meeting started at Yong Wah's basement as usual. We worshiped God and Yong Wah reported. She said that two ladies were coming from Japan and Akemi has invited them for breakfast. That's the way the breakfast gathering was planned.

On the way home, Rita told me that she would cook a quiche, so I just had to prepare tea or coffee. That made me so relieved. I truly thanked her.

On the morning of the 17th, when I came home from shopping, Rita left a message that she would take me shopping. I called her and asked her to take me to a store where I could buy slippers, because I got rid of old guest slippers.

Rita took me to Walmart in the afternoon and I bought two pairs of slippers and some vegetables. I came home and prepared the dining table for the breakfast.

On the 18th of September, I woke up very early and prepared everything very quickly. I made a salad and sliced fresh fruits. Rita arrived with a quiche a little after 8, and we prepared everything, and waited for Yong Wah and the two Japanese ladies to come. We waited until close to 9. Yong Wah had a hard time finding my home. Yong Wah introduced the two Japanese ladies, Yuko and Junko to Rita and me.

We had a very nice breakfast with a delicious quiche and talked and talked.

I asked the Japanese ladies, "How did you become Christians?"

Then Yuko said so naturally, "I met Jesus. He came to me."

"How did you know he was Jesus?" I asked.

"Oh, I attended Christian kindergarten, so I heard about Jesus. When he came to me, he opened his hands wide and smiled at me. I immediately knew he was Jesus."

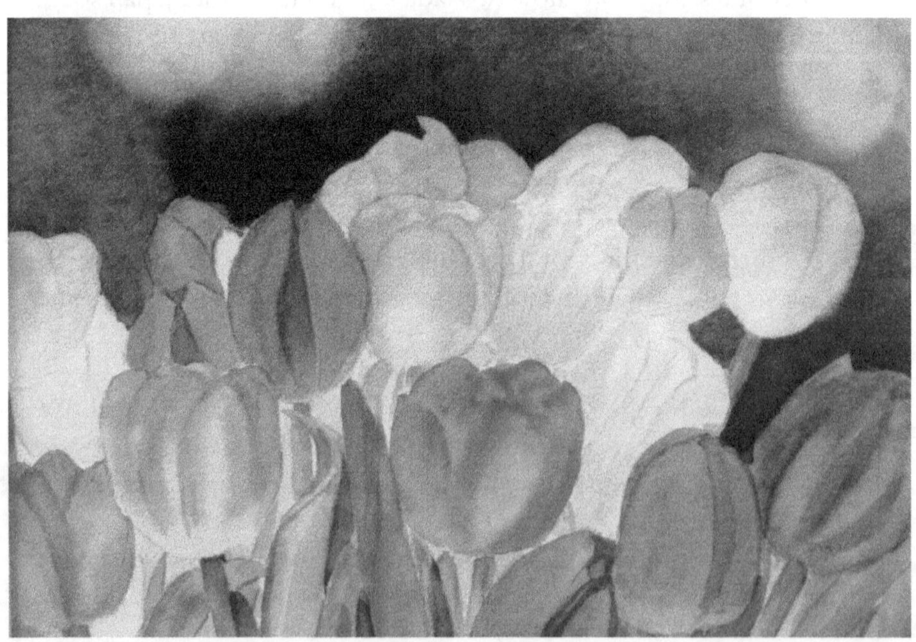

I was so happy to hear that. They also told me that there are so many young people coming to know Jesus, and they are growing so fast."

I received such a blessed report from Yuko and Junko.

We enjoyed being in the garden. The flowers were still blooming beautifully, and the air was warm. We talked a lot and also prayed for each other. They also enjoyed my art gallery tour from the basement to the second floor. I really thanked God that Yong Wah brought the two Japanese ladies, Yuko and Junko, and they told me about Japan. I was truly encouraged and also thanked God.

I thanked God in my heart, "Lord thank you. The Japanese people are coming to know you. I'm so thankful for that. I will continuously pray for Japan."

Yong Wah, Yuko and Junko left around 11:00 o'clock. They drove to Niagara Falls, and planned to attend the conference at the Catch the Fire Toronto church in the evening.

Rita and I cleaned the kitchen and Rita left.

It was quite a busy morning, but it was such a joyful and meaningful morning that God gave me. I truly thanked God and for Rita's kind help!

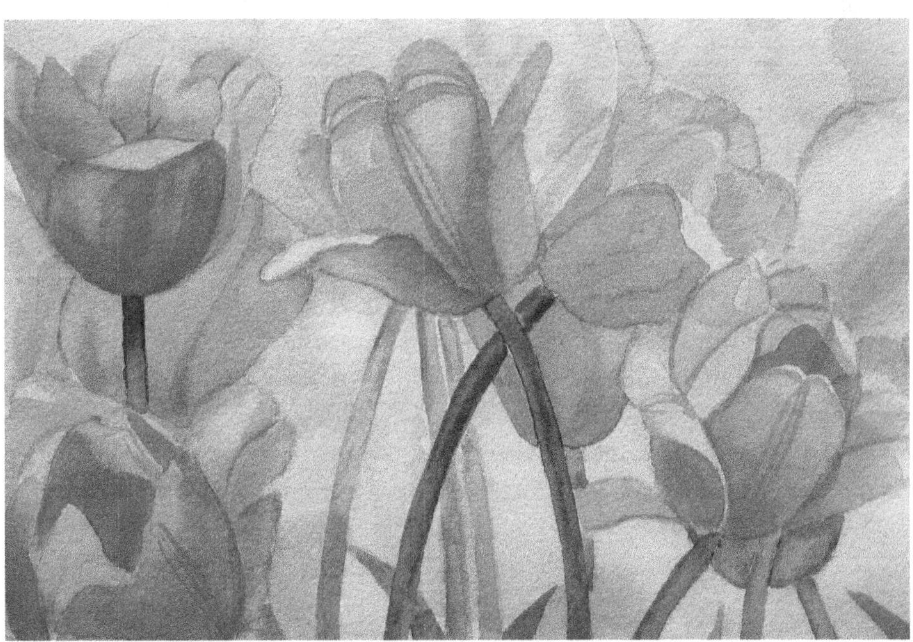

34

October Blessings

October 20, 2019

One afternoon in early October, while I was raking our street, Shirley who lives in front of my house visited me. We said a friendly "Hi" and talked on the street. It was a beautiful, sunny afternoon, and we enjoyed each other's company. When I asked, "How are you?" she said, "Oh, it was terrible. I had a colonoscopy yesterday."

"Oh, that's not comfortable. I am sorry for that," I said.

"I had a very hard time with the preparation. Oh, it was awful," Shirley said.

While we were talking on the street, I remembered my colonoscopy about seven years ago. My family doctor sent me to the colonoscopy clinic. A young doctor examined me. After the examination, the young doctor came to me and said that he removed several polyps from my intestine, and he would send them to a lab. He said that he would call me later and let me know about the results. After a week or two, a lady from the office called me, and I went to see the doctor again. This time the doctor said that my polyps were cancerous, and he wanted to see me in five years. He also told me not to worry about it, because he removed all the polyps. I put the matter in my prayers and visited him after five years. That was two years ago.

At the clinic, the young doctor said to me, "Good to see you. I remember you."

I was really surprised because this doctor examines hundreds of thousands of patients year after year, so it is impossible to remember me.

I said, "No, you have thousands of patients. It's impossible to remember me."

Then he said, "Yes, I do remember you."

That was the way the examination started. After he did my colonoscopy, he came to see me where I was recovering from the anesthesia and said, "Mrs. Tomoda, I don't know how you did it, but it was perfect. You don't have to come and see me anymore."

On the street under the beautiful sun, I told Shirley exactly what happened in my examination two years ago. Then Shirley said, "Because somebody is looking after you, Akemi."

I remember the last part of my experience at the clinic and I told Shirley, "You know I was so happy that I said to the doctor, "Thank you so much, I am so happy," and added, "God bless you."

When the doctor was walking away, he turned to me and said, 'God bless you too.' That's my colonoscopy experience," I said.

We had a wonderful chat on the street in front of my house. I said, "I am so happy to have a neighbour like you. Thank you."

Then Shirley said, "Oh Akemi, you are such a blessing to many of us."

I was so happy to hear that. I don't knock on my neighbours' doors and introduce Jesus, but my desire is that the people on our street would come to know God's love and blessings from my life.

After Shirley left, I enjoyed raking the street again and with thanksgiving in my heart. God used my experience for His glory on our street, and I was so blessed by that.

On the 17th of October, I received a birthday card from Zeny who lives in the Philippines. I met her about 19 years ago. She and her husband Pat, who was a pastor, visited their son and his family on our street. Then she found out that I lost my husband and visited me to comfort me. We talked in my living room. She quoted many Bible verses in her conversation and prayed over me. I thanked her and prayed over her, then she started crying and said, "Can I come and see you one more time with my husband?"

"Of course, you can," I said.

Then one afternoon, Zeny and her husband Pat visited me, and we talked. I don't recall anything we talked about, but they enjoyed their visit and invited me to the Philippines.

"If you visit Japan, please visit us to."

I thanked them too. Since then Zeny has sent me letters and a birthday card every year. I received many letters from her. Eventually she lost her husband too.

I did not write many letters, but I kept on sending her my hand-painted cards and she liked them.

The last few months, Zeny sent me many letters with many prayer requests. She wrote that somebody started gossiping about her church, and the church was divided. Since this church was established by her husband, she worried about the future of her church. Zeny sent me many letters to pray for her church.

I prayed with my friend Rita, every time I received one of her letters. I sensed Zeny's deep worry and even fear about her church.

Finally, I decided to write a letter to her. I wrote that this church is God's church, and God knows everything that is going on in the church more than she knows. I also wrote that I was praying that God's best will be done in the situation. I wrote that "In all things God works for the good of those who love him," and I included this situation in all things and expect good results will come. I also wrote that God is changing her and the people in her church into the likeness of his son Jesus, through difficulty and hardship. "He is making you overcomers sit with Him in heavenly places."

I sent this letter with my hand-painted card.

Later I received a letter in a birthday card to me. In it Zeny wrote:

Dear Akemi,

Your letters and the personalized card you sent lighten our heartaches over the experiences of these past months, and even cheers, our pastor and his wife, who is also a pastor were both amazed at your painting. She celebrated her birthday on September 13 and asked for one of your paintings, which she hangs on our wall as her gift.

You have been a blessing to me since the day we, Pat and I, first met you, and now you have blessed our pastors also.

May God continually bless you in every way and give power to your prayers as well. May He keep you safe and secure in whatever you do and wherever you go. May He give His Angels charge over you to keep you in all your ways.

Much love in Jesus,

Zeny

When I read this letter, I truly thanked God for using me, my letter and even my painting for his purpose in the Philippines, and I was so blessed by that.

I said to God, "Thank you Lord, you can even use my letter. I am so blessed. Use me for your glory more and more."

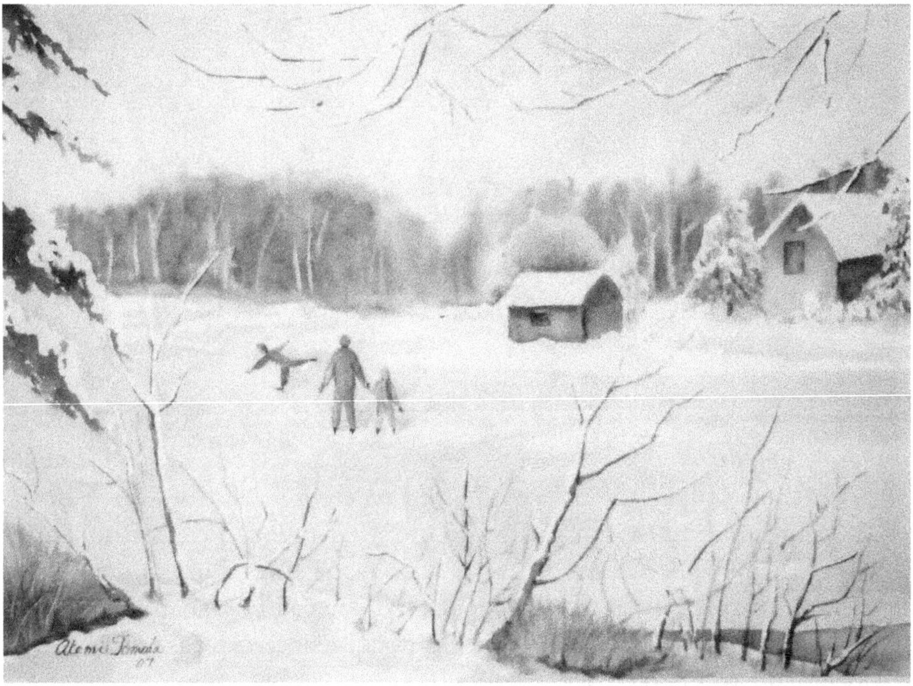

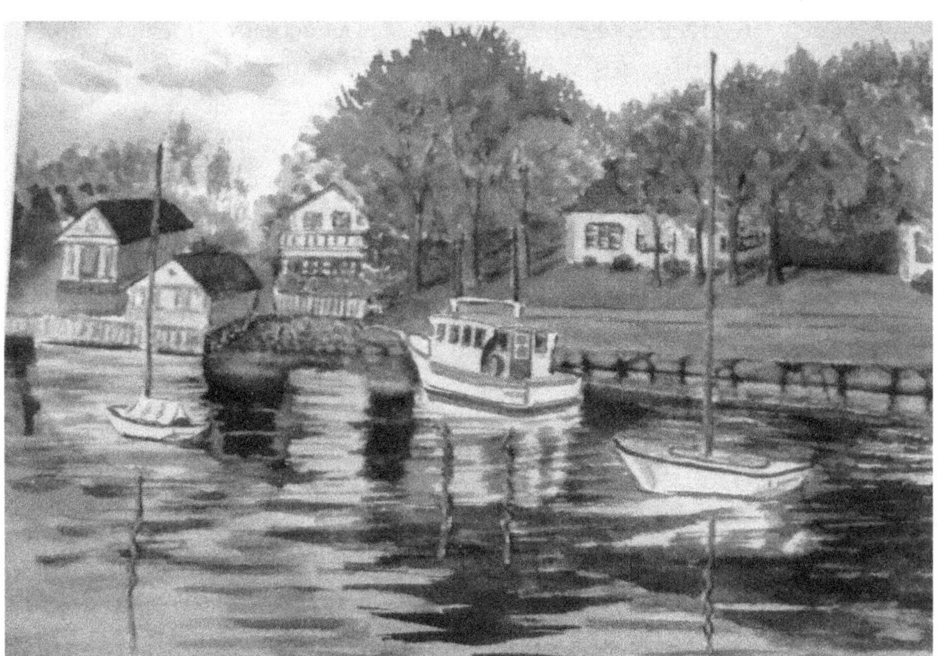

35

I Changed My Will

November 13, 2019

At the beginning of the year 2019, I received a call from Mr. Gordon Fukushima, the trustee of my sister-in-law, Yaye Saisho. He said, "Akemi, your name is in Yaye's will. Yaye's sister, Fusako, and her two sons' names are in the will too. Could you call Fusako and tell her about this? Also, I will send you the documents, so please send the documents to Fusako too."

I said, "Of course I will. Thank you for looking after this."

When I heard this unexpected news, I was actually shocked, because I never expected that Yaye would put my name in her will. It touched my heart deeply, not because of the money I will receive, but of her kindness and love for me. I called Fusako in Japan and mentioned about Yaye's will. Soon I received the documents for Fusako, her two sons, and me, and I sent the three documents to Japan.

While I was going through the process, I thought about Yaye and her kind heart towards us. Her caring heart and her love spoke loudly through her well. Suddenly, I wanted to do the same as Yaye did, and wanted to change my will, including more people to share my love and my thankful heart towards them after my death.

I thought about it often, and also prayed about it. Eventually I had a clear idea what to change and how to change it. I wrote it down on the paper and filed it and forgot it for a long time.

Spring came and the perennials started growing. When I was in the garden, suddenly the thought of changing my will came back to me so strongly, and also, I wanted to do it during this year. Before when I always drove my car, everything was very easy, but now it is not easy like before. I have to call a taxi or ask my friend to take me there. I thought about it, but the more I thought about it the more it felt so complicated. I said to God in the spring garden, "Father, I need your help. Please help me. I would like to change my will, and also, I would like to change it before the end of this year. Thank you."

I put everything about changing my will into God's hand and was relieved.

Since then nothing happened for a long time.

We had lots of rain in the spring and also in the summer, and the perennials grew so much and bloomed with almost double the number of flowers. Since the year 2000, when my husband moved to heaven, I have looked after the garden for 20 years, but this year was the best year for the garden. So many flowers bloomed, and the Lord's garden was so glorious, and I enjoyed it so much in the garden, and I thanked God a lot every day.

In early October, Janis visited me. While we were talking, she said "Akemi, your birthday is coming, but I don't know what to give to you."

Then suddenly the changing of my will came to mind and I said, "Could you help me to change my will? That would be the best birthday gift for me."

"Of course, I will do that," she said.

"Thank you. I wanted to change it by the end of this year." I was so relieved and also so happy.

At the end of October, Janis called me and asked me which day I was free and made an appointment with the Streetsville Law Office on the 30th of October at 11.

On the 30th of October, Janis came and drove me to the Streetsville Law Office, and I asked the lawyer Mr. Ayub Azam Ali to change my will. He agreed with my request and also changed the arrangement of my Power of Attorney, Janis and Gary, because Gary had moved far away. The lawyer suggested that Janis can act by herself now. He said that he would do it quickly, and I could pick it up the following week. Janis drove me home, and I was so happy.

After Janis left, I went out into the fall garden and looked at the red leaves on the gate of heaven. I thanked God for answering my request. "Father, thank you for your help. My will is going to be changed soon. I am so pleased. Thank you so much."

This year, very cold weather is expected in November, so that afternoon I started cutting the perennial stems. I cut a lot and put them into yard waste bags. I made three full bags of perennials, except the ones still blooming. My backyard looks so empty, but I like to clean in the fall rather than next spring.

On the 6th of November, Janis drove me again to the lawyer's office to pick up my will. We talked and the lawyer explained what he did for my will, and I signed the papers, also two witnesses signed the paper. I paid the fee and Janis and I walked to Janis' car.

In her car, Janis asked me, "Do you want to go somewhere, Akemi? I can take you."

I said, "Would you take me to Shoppers Drug Mart? I would like to pick up my prescription."

"Of course, I can."

We went to Shoppers Drug Mart and I picked up my prescription for my knee pain. Then we went to Tim Horton's and we ate lunch with a cup of tea. Janis drove me home. It was about 1:30 PM. When Janis was leaving from my driveway, she said to me, "Happy birthday, Akemi."

I was really thankful for Janis' wonderful birthday gift. I was able to change my will this year.

That afternoon I raked the backyard neatly and picked up thousands and thousands of maple tree seeds. So many trees still have leaves, but I sensed that I had to clean it before it's too late. I spent more than 2 1/2 hours in the garden and picked up three yard waste bags of dead leaves, and vacuumed the seeds with the lawnmower. I cleaned the Lord's garden neatly and I was so satisfied and thanked God that I was able to do it again this year.

After I finished cleaning the garden, I came back into the house and sat on the living room sofa, and thanked God officially.

"Father, thank you. I wanted to change my will so badly within this year, and I was able to do that because of Janis' great help. I am so thankful and happy for that. Father, I also thank you that I was able to look after your garden this year again. Oh, what a wonderful time I spent in your garden this summer. Thank you, I am so grateful that I can ask you. You are a wonderful father. Thank you again."

I am so glad I cleaned the garden. The next week, we had about 15 centimeters of snow on the 11th of November.

36

The Celebration of Marlene's Life

December 3, 2019

Early in the morning of November 11th, I received a long-distance call. When I said, "Hello," a man said, "Hi Akemi, this is Glen. I am the son of Marlene Traas."

"Hi Glen. Are you visiting Canada now?"

I asked because Glen lives in New Zealand. Then he said, "Yes, I am in Oakville now. Could you visit my mom soon? She stopped eating and she is in a critical condition. Have you visited her recently?"

"No, I could not, because I don't drive a car anymore. But I will ask my friend to visit your mother."

"Thank you. I appreciate that," Glen said.

Marlene Traas is living in a senior's home in Oakville. A couple of years ago, she came back from New Zealand and started living there.

About a year ago, Rita drove me there and we visited Marlene. She remembered me but did not remember Rita anymore. We talked and had a good time. Marlene forgot so many things at that time, but her passion for the Lord did not change at all. She prayed beautiful prayers to God, and I truly enjoyed praying with her. Since then I could not visit her.

I called Rita and mentioned about Marlene's condition, and asked her if she could drive me there again, because Rita was busy preparing to visit Israel on the 18th of November.

She said, "Yes I can drive you there. When would you like to go?"

"How about on the 15th, Friday afternoon?"

"Okay. Let's do it."

I truly thanked Rita for her kind help.

I soon called Violet Royed too. She is a very close friend of Marlene and lives very close to her. I mentioned Marlene's condition and asked her to visit Marlene soon. Then Violet said that she would visit her as soon as possible. I looked forward to visiting Marlene and was excited about it.

Then the next day I received a call from Violet. She said, "Akemi, Marlene passed away today."

"What?"

"I called Pat, Marlene's stepdaughter, and she said that Marlene passed away this morning. When I know about her funeral, I will let you know."

I really thanked Violet. On that day, I also found a message on my phone from Glen. He also mentioned Marlene's death. I called Rita and told her of Marlene's death.

A few days later Violet called me again and told me that Marlene's funeral would be held on the 18th of November at Bethel Christian Reformed Church in Waterdown. I asked her if I could not find anyone to drive me there, would she give me a ride, and she said yes.

One day before the funeral, I called Janis Flowers, my trustee, and asked if she would attend Marlene's funeral, and she said that she wasn't planning to do that. But soon she called me back, and decided to attend the funeral, and said she could drive me there. I was so pleased and thanked her.

On the 18th of November, Janis drove me to Bethel Christian Church in Waterdown. It was a rainy day and very foggy, but we arrived at the church safely.

While Janis was looking for a place to park her car, I walked into the church and a man welcomed me. While I was hanging up my jacket, a lady approached me and said, "You must be Akemi, right?"

"Yes, I am," I said. I had never seen this lady before.

Then she said, "I was a prayer partner with Marlene. Every time I visited and prayed with her, she said she wanted to pray for Akemi. So, I know you."

"Thank you for telling me. That's really wonderful to know. I also prayer for Marlene every morning," I said.

Then the lady said, "You know Marlene knew she was going home in this year. She said to me, "I'm going home within this year," and the next time I visited her, she said, "Three more weeks to go," and the last time that I visited her, she could not speak. She painted out heaven with her finger and passed away soon afterwards."

I really thanked the lady who told me this beautiful story.

Soon the ceremony started. About 50 people got together and celebrated Marlene's beautiful life with God with many songs and good messages. The scripture was read from Mark 10: 35-45.

"For even, the Son of Man came not to be served but to serve, and give his life as a ransom for many."

Many people gave testimonies of Marlene's wonderful influence in their lives. Marlene introduced Jesus to many people, and also helped them to grow in God's love.

While I was listening to the many testimonies, I remembered how she had helped in my life. She was a leader of a Bible study group. One day, I came home from the Bible study, then soon Marlene and Violet visited me at my house and baptized me with the Holy Spirit. I was truly shocked for her kindness. When I lost my husband, she visited me and stayed overnight at my home, and the next day she drove me to a funeral home to arrange my husband's funeral. It was so intense. I had to decide so many things so quickly, but she helped me so wonderfully.

Marlene also encouraged me to write essays, and she typed my essays and made them into booklets. She made booklets of my essays. I was able to keep my essays, and later published my books.

Marlene was such a faithful woman, and I enjoyed listening to the many testimonies. We were all so pleased that we had met Marlene and could celebrate her life here on earth. I sensed that there was a big celebration in heaven to welcome Marlene too. God is so pleased with her life and is welcoming her into a beautiful mansion.

After the funeral, Glen came to me and said, "Akemi, thank you for coming. I'm so glad to meet you again. This is a book I made about my mother. Please keep one." He gave me a book of Marlene's photographic life history.

I told him how much Marlene had helped me in my life, and I'm so thankful to have her in my life.

We had a nice gathering with good food and talked more about Marlene's life.

Janis drove me home and I truly thanked God that I had met Marlene. She helped me a lot and also prayed for me a lot. Now I feel that Marlene is still praying for me from heaven. Suddenly I started feeling that heaven is much closer to me, and truly excited that I will see her again in heaven.

37

Precious Christmas gift

December 20, 2019

This year 2019, I celebrated Christmas and the birth of Jesus in so many ways. Our church, Life House Church, had many Christmas gatherings. The ladies Christmas dinner, "The Best Gift Ever" was held on the 30th of November at the church office. Eighty ladies gathered and celebrated the birth of Jesus with singing Christmas carols, listening to many good testimonies, and eating a delicious meal. I enjoyed spending time with my sisters in the Lord very much.

On the 5th of December, our prayer group held a Christmas lunch at the Mandarin. Seven ladies had a happy gathering with Chinese food. I enjoyed having a Christmas lunch with my prayer mates.

On the evening of the 14th of December, our home group had a Christmas dinner at the church office, and about 20 people got together, and celebrated a very nice Christmas gathering with delicious food, games, and encouraging prayers. I sensed the presence of God in the gathering and enjoyed being there so much.

When Anne Hanson drove me home, I truly thanked God for the way I was celebrating the birth of Jesus with my brothers and sisters in so many ways. These were wonderful gifts from God. I was overwhelmed by God's gifts for us. He gave his son to be born in a manger and lived on the earth and died on the cross to give us true life. While I was thanking God for His kind gifts, my telephone rang. When I answered, "Hello," a lady said, "Hi Akemi, I am Kaoru. Do you remember me?"

"Kaoru Urano?" I asked.

"Yes, that's me. I am in Barrie now, and I will go back to Japan in three days, but I would like to see you tomorrow. Is that okay?"

"Tomorrow I am going to church."

"Then I will go to church with you."

"Can you come before 10, because my friend is giving me a ride, and she will be here around 10."

"Yes, I can. I will be at your house before 10. See you tomorrow," she replied.

I was truly surprised by Kaoru but was excited to see her. Kaoru had visited me twice in the past. The first time she visited, my husband Ken was still alive, and the second time she visited me, I was alone. This is going to be the third visit. I took a bath, and thanked God for the beautiful day I spent, and went to bed.

The next morning, I prepared myself to attend church, and a little before 10:00 AM, Kaoru came with her two Japanese friends. They dropped Kaoru at my house and drove to Niagara Falls.

Kaoru and I greeted each other and waited for Sharon to come to drive us to the church. While we were waiting, Kaoru said that she and another lady came to Barrie with 12 Japanese high school students for an exchange students' program. Twelve students are in Canada for two weeks, but she and another teacher are staying here for only four days, and she told me that she is a principal of Onomichi Higashi High School. I was really shocked and also so happy to hear that!

Sharon came and drove us to the church, and we attended the Sunday service. We worshipped God together and listened to the message, which was delivered by our home group leader, Mohit, who was a pastor in India before.

After the service, my good friend Selina came to me. I introduced Kaoru to her and asked her to bless Kaoru, and she prayed over her. Selina is a very faithful lady, and she was also a pastor. Kaoru speaks good English, and we had a good time together.

Sharon drove us home, and we ate lunch together. Fortunately, I had some delicious chicken soup which my dear friend Anita brought me a few days before. We enjoyed eating chicken soup and apple salad. While we were eating, Kaoru said, "This is my third visit to you, to this house, but you haven't changed. You look so happy."

"Thank you. God is good to me. He is helping me a lot," I said.

Kaoru said, "I remember the first time I came. It was 33 years ago, and your husband was alive. You helped me a lot. You cooked Japanese food for me. And your husband drove me to Niagara Falls. The second time I came here was 16 years ago. That time you were alone, but helped me a lot, and I was able to continue my life. This time I don't have any problems. I just want to say thank you for your help. I am a principal of Hiroshima Prefectural High School now."

I congratulated her. It is truly wonderful the way she is living now. I remembered her two visits to us clearly too.

The first time, she was an exchange University student in Albany NY, but she could not handle it well, and wanted to quit and go back to Japan. Her mother sent a letter to Ken and me to take her for a week, and Kaoru came to spend an Easter week with us. During the week, somehow, she was restored and went back to Albany, and finished her course, and went back to Japan, and she became a high school teacher.

The second time she visited me, I was alone. I could not take her anywhere, but I prayed over her and encouraged her. I remembered at that time she invited Jesus into her heart and went back to Japan knowing that God would go with her.

Now she is a principal. I believe I blessed her future in my prayers, but I never thought that God would bless her that much. I was truly thankful for Kaoru's third visit with her wonderful report.

After lunch, Kaoru took out her gifts for me and shared with me about her high school. After I received her gifts, I took her upstairs, where I keep my paintings and showed her several of my paintings, and said, "If you like, you can choose one." She chose one and said, "Can I have two?"

"Sure, if you like," I said.

She picked two paintings, saying, "Can I have one for my mother?"

"Yes, you can."

Kaoru picked three paintings. Then her friends came back from Niagara Falls. I invited them into my house and offered them a cup of tea and some snacks.

They stayed for awhile and left with Kaoru before 3:00 o'clock. Kaoru was with me only five hours, but I truly thanked God for showing me how Kaoru is doing now, and how the seed we, Ken and I, sowed 33 years ago is growing and blossoming beautifully now. It was an awesome gift for the Christmas season! I truly thanked God and asked him to use me for his glory more and more. I have been spending this Christmas time with his wonderful gifts, but the best gift is that he gave His Son Jesus to be born in a manger. Also, the same Jesus was born into our hearts. What amazing lives we have! I truly thanked God for that.

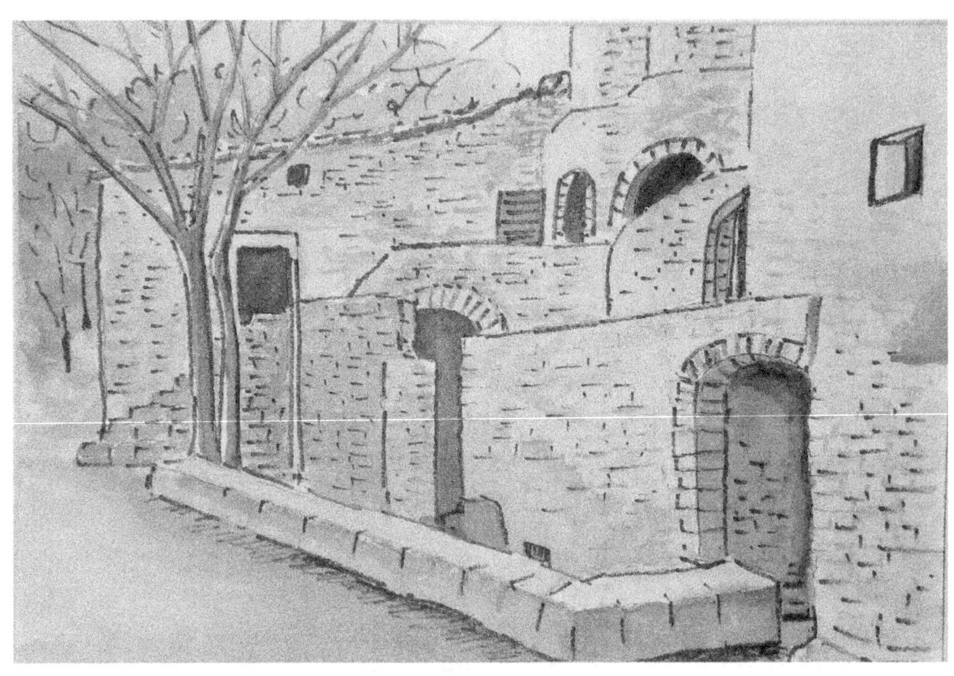

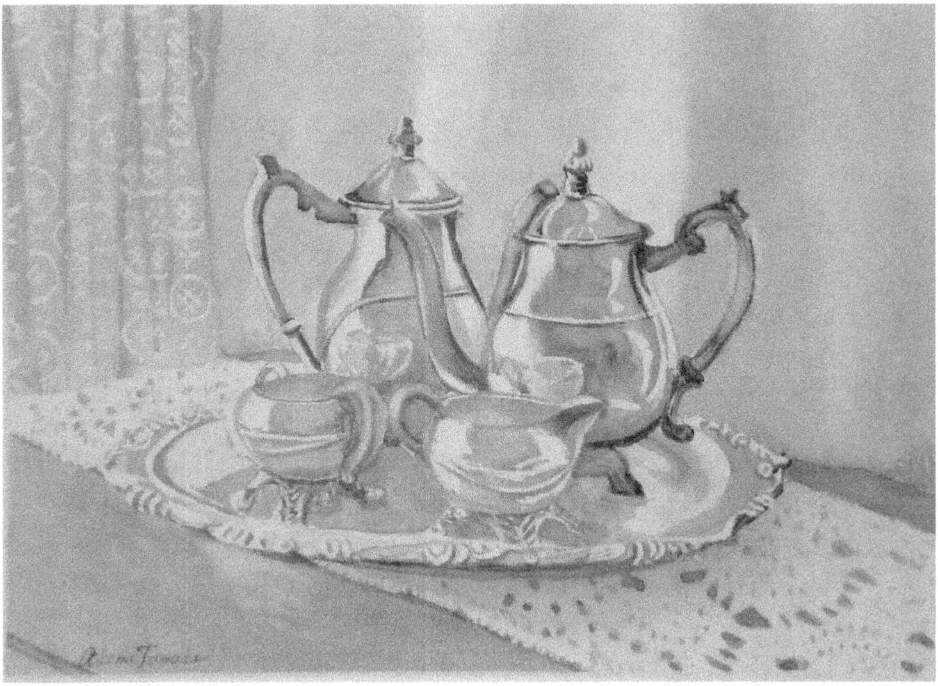

38

The Year 2020 Started

January 20, 2020

In the last year 2019, the Lord emphasized to me to clean the temple of God, to remove my desires, my aims, my goals, and put Him first instead, His desires, His aims, and His goals for my life. God was saying to me, "Let me live my life fully through you."

I felt so awesome to live my life with God, and the year 2019 ended beautifully with so many gatherings to celebrate Jesus' birth with lots of thanksgiving and praise.

The new year 2020 started with a big expectation for the new decade and the new year, and I was so thrilled to be able to live this new year with God.

One day early this year, when I was reading the Bible, Luke 22:42 hit me so strongly, and I knew that God was telling me to use it in my life.

Luke 22:42 says:

"Father, if you are willing to take this cup from me; yet not my will, but yours be done."

God was saying to me, "Let's go together, this new year with holding hands tightly. I want you to ask for my will in every situation and every circumstance."

I felt so awesome and thanked God for my precious journey with God. But it is a very serious matter. God wants me to look at Him all the time and trust Him fully in every situation and every circumstance, knowing that His ways are higher than my ways and His thoughts are higher than mine. I wondered what was waiting for me in the year 2020, because I was facing a totally new chapter in my life.

The year 2020 started with wonderful news from Malaysia. One day in early January, my friend Janette's sister, Angela, called me from Malaysia and said, "Akemi, Happy New Year! This is Angela."

"Happy New Year to you," I said.

Then she said, "Akemi, I have good news. I am totally free from cancer. Thank you for your prayers, and I wanted to tell you this good news."

"Thank you for telling me. I am so happy for you. God is good. He is so good. Isn't He?"

"Yes, God is good. Akemi, would you pray for me in this new year?"

"Of course, I will pray for you," I said, and I prayed that Angela would have a beautiful life with God in the year 2020. I asked God to bless Angela abundantly, and that she would have a victorious life with God in this year. Angela also prayed over me and blessed me. We had a good time talking on the phone.

I met Angela many years ago while she was visiting Canada. Janette asked me to teach Angela how to paint watercolours, so I gave her lessons a few times. She went back to Malaysia, but she called me often and asked me to pray for her healing. I am so glad about what God did for Angela and asked that His will would be done in Angela's life. This year started so wonderfully, and I thanked God for that.

Since I've stopped driving a car, I changed my dentist to the closest one. I can walk there in five minutes. But this winter I had to change my appointment, because it was too cold to walk. I made a new appointment on the 13th of January, and I found out that we would have so much snow on the 11th, so I decided to change the appointment again. When I mentioned this to my friend, Rita Gervais, she said "Don't change it. I will take you there, and also take you to do your grocery shopping." She took me to the dentist and also for grocery shopping too.

On the 14th of January, another friend Anita Khan, drove me to DeSerres, an art supply store and I bought many things, a few frames, mats, and watercolour papers. I was so happy to do that, and Anita helped me to carry my art supplies into my house. We prayed together in my living room.

On the 20th of January, close to 9:00 PM, Daniel Hoogsteen called me. He said, "Hi Akemi, this is Daniel. The other day my mom forced you to say "yes" to our offer. We want to bring cooked food for you. Could we come now?"

"Now? It's late. Is it okay with you?"

"Yes. We won't stay long. We will see you soon," Daniel said.

Daniel and I met at Christian Reformed Church about 20 years ago. Then he was a little boy, and we sat together at the church every Sunday and enjoyed making origami. We left that church, but I kept on sending him a birthday card.

One day before Christmas, Daniel and his father Doug, visited me with a huge poinsettia as a Christmas gift. While we were talking in my living room, Doug asked me, "How are you doing? Are you alright?"

I said, "I am good. I still enjoy painting, writing, even sewing, but I don't enjoy cooking anymore. Cooking for myself day after day is not fun at all!"

Then a few days later, Daniel's mother Nanette, called me and said, "Akemi, we want to bring some cooked food for you. You just warm it up in a microwave and eat it. Okay?"

I was so shocked to hear that and said, "No, no, don't do that. I can still look after myself. Please don't do that. Also, I don't use a microwave oven. It's not good for my nervous system. Please don't do that."

After I talked to Nan, I truly regretted what I said to Doug, and decided that I would never mention it again.

Then only a week later, Nan called me again and said, "Akemi, this is Nan. I know what you said, but we would really like to bring some food for you, because we love you. Please let us do this. You don't have to use a microwave oven. You can steam them to eat. We helped my mother-in-law in that way. Please let us do that. Okay?"

I said, "Thank you for your kindness." I could not say no to her anymore.Soon Daniel and his mother arrived with six packages of home cooked frozen food in a bag, and said, "If you don't like any of them, let us know. We want to bring what you like."

I was so stunned. They had brought so much food for me. They were nicely packed in small containers and the name of the food was written on the paper lids.

I truly thanked them, and also thanked God who brought these loving people into my life.

Since God wanted me to ask for only His will this year, I never asked any of them, yet He poured out His blessings on my life. His blessings were overflowing on me. I started this year 2020 with such an awesome feeling to know more and more about the depth of God's love for His children. I am truly thankful to live this life with God.

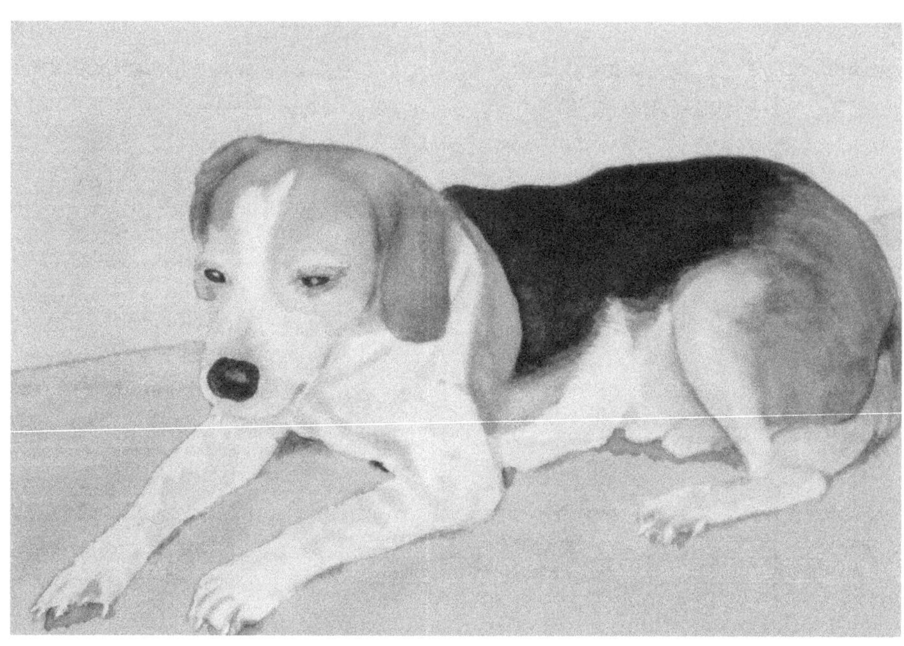

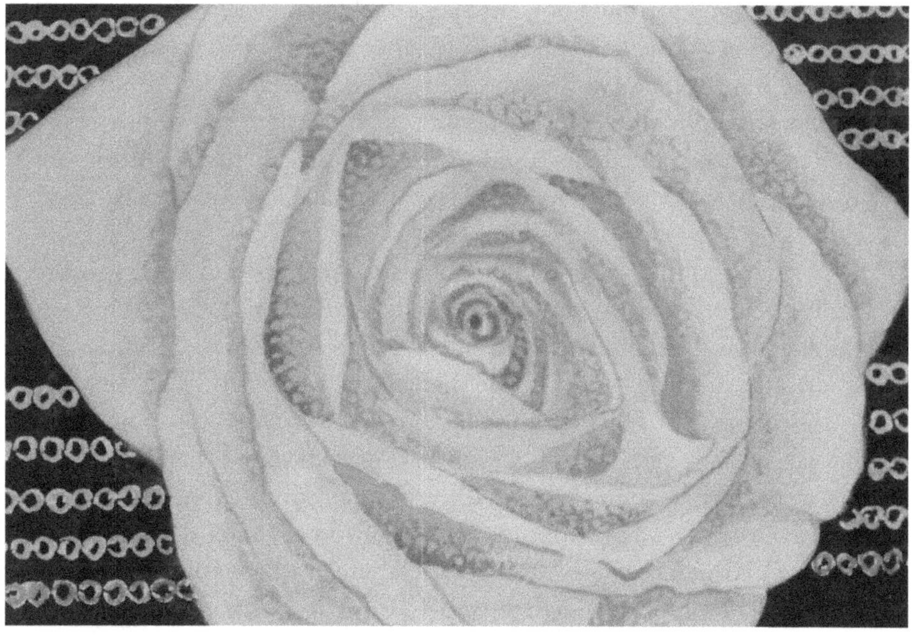

39

Our Precious Gathering

February 22, 2020

I had a precious lunch gathering with my three friends on the 20th of February at my house. Rita Gervais, Heather Casuel, and Janice Orr visited me with home cooked food, and we had a precious gathering with a delicious lunch, good conversation and also prayers.

Exactly 20 years ago, right after my husband's death, my friend Rita visited me once a week and prayed over me. Every time she prayed, God gave her a picture and I received tremendous encouragement from her prayers. Rita visited me once a week for more than half a year and prayed for me. Soon she started taking me to her home group at the Toronto Airport church. People met once a week on Friday evenings at Bill and Sue Dupley's house in Mississauga.

I wasn't a member of that church, but people received me, and I felt very comfortable being there. I received lots of healing from that group, and also hoped to live my life continually in such blessed company.

In that group, I met many wonderful brothers and sisters in the Lord. Everyone was so serious about being a child of God. That encouraged me so much, and I learned so much from them. Heather and Janice were in that group, and we met once a week faithfully.

Then one day Heather came to me and invited me to join them and eat lunch together once a month. She mentioned that Janice and Rita were in the group. I thanked her for her kind invitation, and we started gathering once a month, bringing food together. I enjoyed the gathering so much, since I was totally alone, and ate food by myself every day. It was a nice change, and I also enjoyed the delicious food the ladies brought. I don't remember which year we started this gathering, but probably 15 or 16 years ago, and we are still meeting once a month faithfully. Recently Heather said that at the first gathering, we celebrated my birthday, so it must have started in October.

Since then we have been meeting once a month for so many years, month after month, year after year. We really enjoyed eating such delicious food together and talking about the blessing of God in our lives and prayed for each other. It is such a precious gathering!

February the 20th, we had a lunch gathering at my home. In the morning, I prepared the dining table putting the tablecloth, table placemats and napkins, knives and forks, and glasses out. While I was preparing the table, I felt warmness in my heart and truly enjoyed doing that. I said in my heart, "Father, thank you. I'm able to prepare the table for a group gathering. I'm so happy to do that. Thank you for giving me such faithful ladies as my friends, and they are visiting me in my house. Father, join us when we get together, and bless us abundantly. Thank you."

I sensed that God was excited about our gathering and smiling at me. It was truly awesome, and I thought we will meet together for many more years and enjoy each other's company.

Around noon, Rita called me and said, "Akemi, I will be a little late. I had a technical difficulty. I will be at your home in 20 minutes."

"Thank you for telling me. See you soon," I said.

Late afternoon, Janice and Heather came in Janice's car. Janice brought cooked vegetables and Heather brought a cake. I mentioned to them about Rita's delay. While we were arranging the food on the table, and I took my salads out from the fridge, Rita came with a roast chicken, and told us that her oven did not work properly. When she sliced the chicken it wasn't fully cooked, so we put it into my oven to finish cooking.

We waited about 30 minutes talking to each other. Then suddenly a thought came to me that it would be so nice to have communion together. So, I went to the living room and took out a communion plate and four small glasses, and poured wine into them and put a cracker on the plate, and invited them to the living room. Our gathering started with communion this time, eating the body of Christ and drinking the blood of Christ. It was so beautiful, and I enjoyed it so much! Then Janice started praying for healing over Heather, who suffered the flu recently. So, we all prayed over her for good health and many blessings of God over her and her family.

Meanwhile the chicken was ready, and we sat on the dining chairs, and enjoyed a delicious lunch together with friendly conversation.

The last 15 years, we all had problems and difficulties in our lives, yet we kept on meeting, helping each other and encouraging each other. It is so wonderful to see the way we have been growing in the Lord.

After lunch, we cleaned up the dishes and sat on the sofa and prayed.

Heather read Isaiah 61:1-3

"The spirit of sovereign Lord is in me, because the Lord has anointed me to preach good news to the poor….to comfort all who mourn, and provide for those who grieve in Zion… to bestow on them a crown of beauty instead of ashes, the oil of gladness instead of mourning and a garment of praise instead of spirit of despair. They will be called oaks of righteousness, a planting of the Lord for the display of His splendour.

Then we prayed for China, where many people are suffering from coronavirus. We prayed for healing and declared that God is bigger and stronger than this unfortunate situation. We prayed that God message will spread further and wider than the virus and many people will be saved in China, Asia, and all over the world. We declared a year of great harvest for the year 2020.

Rita received a picture from God and told us that God was giving us a big sword to fight against enemies. We also discussed the importance of true love and true humility for our lives.

We set our next meeting for the 19th of March and finished our meeting with lots of thanksgiving in our hearts.

After the ladies left, I truly thanked God for the wonderful time we spent at my house and how God joined us in a wonderful way. I looked forward to meeting them again on the 19th of March. I truly desire to meet together continually for many more years.

40

I Received My Message

March 22, 2020

Several years ago, when I was attending Catch the Fire Mississauga Church, one Sunday we had a guest speaker, prophetess, Isabel Allum. After she delivered her message, she and her two helpers prophesied over everyone of us. At that time, Isabel prophesied over me, and said, "I see a picture of you. You are blowing a big horn. God will give you a message to tell the people."

I was very excited about it and wanted to know what kind of message God would give me. But I did not get any particular message from God and years went by. I totally forgot about the prophecy.

The end of last year, our prayer group leader, Sharon Hancie at Lifehouse Church asked me to tell our group my message.

She said, "It does not have to be a long message, I just want to know what God is telling you."

I took it seriously and started thinking about it. What kind of message could I deliver to the ladies in our prayer group? One day I asked God about it. I said, "Father, I need your help. I have to deliver a message to the ladies in our prayer group. What kind of message should I deliver?"

Then God said to me, "Tell them what you learned from your life."

I thought about it seriously. My life has not been an easy one. I went through many valleys and difficulties. I could not have gone through them without God's help. I shed lots of tears and cried a lot when I lost my husband from a massive heart attack.

One day I cried to God and said, "Father, I am in a blazing furnace. Help me. If you fail to help me, I can't survive." Then God helped me by sending me many wonderful people and carried me through safely.

I suffered a lot, but God was with me. He never left me nor forsook me. I realized that this was my message and thanked God.

One day while I was thinking about the blazing furnace in my life, Daniel Chapter 3 came to me, so I read it and thought about it. Daniel's three friends, Shadrach, Meshach and Abednego were cast into the blazing furnace by Nebuchadnezzar, because they refused to worship idols.

While I was reading the story, suddenly God started speaking to me.

"Don't you think I could extinguish the fire?"

"Yes, you could," I said.

"But I did not. Don't you think I could remove people from the blazing furnace miraculously?" God said.

"Yes, you could," I said.

"But I did not. I was with them in the blazing furnace and protected them," God said.

"Yes, you did," I said. Then God said to me, "Not only these three friends of Daniel, but also I am with all my children. No matter how hard their lives are I never leave them nor forsake them. I am with them and protected them."

That was a truly encouraging message from God, and I was so thankful for that.

Another time while I was thinking about my difficult life, I read Genesis 39 again. Joseph did not do anything wrong, but he was put in a prison. While I was reading carefully, Genesis 39: 21-23 hit me so strong.

Genesis 39: 20-21

"But while Joseph was there in the prison, the Lord was with him: he showed him kindness and granted him favours in the eyes of the prison warden.

Genesis 39: 23

"The warden paid no attention to anything under Joseph's care, because the Lord was with Joseph and gave him success in whatever he did. Joseph went through very hard times, but God was with him and showed him kindness and favour. God used this opportunity to save the Israelites from famine.

When I read this, I believed that this is my message from God.

"Sometimes we go through very difficult times, but we will never be alone. God goes with us. He never leaves us nor forsakes us."

I prepared my message and wrote it down in my notebook about God's part.

1. He never leaves us nor forsakes us. He is with us always.
2. He is faithful and keeps his promises.
3. He can use anything for good.

I also wrote down about our part.

1. We must look at God all the times and don't look at our problems, otherwise we will be burned.
2. Trust God completely. No matter how difficult our problem is God is bigger than that, and trust that His way is higher than our ways and His thoughts are higher than us.
3. Thank God.

In all things God works good for those who love him, who had been called according to his purpose. When I wrote down these messages, I truly believed that this is the message God gave to me, and I remember the prophecy I received from Isabel Allum many years ago, and thanked God for that.

One Thursday in January, I delivered this message to the ladies in our prayer group and thanked God for it.

Now I have a message from God. I would like to encourage many Christians who are going through a very difficult time by telling them that "You are not alone. God is with you. He knows everything you are experiencing. He will help you and deliver you."

Now we are having a very difficult time with coronavirus. It is spreading all over the world. Schools are closed, churches are closed, meetings are cancelled, and many people are staying home. One day I called my friend, Dianne Schleifer and talked about the situation, then she said, "Akemi, read Psalm 91. I found this from the Internet." I thanked her and opened my Bible to Psalm 91.

About 20 years ago, I memorized Psalm 91 and wrote it down on a paper. When I opened my Bible, I found the old tiny paper. When I opened the tiny paper, I was able to read, "I will be with him in trouble, I will deliver him and honour him."

When I read this, I truly thanked God for showing me again and again that this is His message for me. Now I have a message from God.

We are facing a very difficult time with coronavirus now, but we are not alone. God is always with us, and he is bigger than this. We will have victory over this situation!

41

Under a Global Pandemic

April 5, 2020

Coronavirus started spreading in China only a couple of months ago, and now it has spread all over the world. Every day the number of patients and the number of deaths has increased. Already 1 million people are affected by it. All schools are closed, and children are staying home everyday. Churches are closed, and we don't get together to worship God anymore. All meetings are cancelled, and many stores are closed. It is so big and spreading so fast! We are all housebound. I stopped taking a bus to do my shopping. We are told to keep a physical distance from other people, and people over 70 years of age are told not to go out at all.

My life is not easy now. I can't go grocery shopping or visit a pharmacy or even go to a bank by myself. Without my friends help I can't survive. I don't know how long it will last, but it's not an easy time to live.

I experienced World War Two when I was a little girl, but we were able to go to school everyday, and people were able to gather together and encourage each other. The coronavirus totally isolates everybody. Not many cars are running on the roads and stores are so empty.

After I stopped driving my car, I started taking a bus for my shopping, and I enjoyed it, sitting on a bus and relaxing. It took me to Meadowvale Town Centre in 10 minutes. I did not have to check to the left or to the right, and also the busy traffic. I was able to go to my bank, my doctor, my pharmacy and grocery store. I truly enjoyed the freedom of going out by myself when I wanted.

Recently many of my friends called me and warned me not to take the bus anymore. It's too dangerous, and also, they suggested not to do grocery shopping anymore. I did not know what to do. I simply cannot live like that. I was in trouble.

One morning, I just went out to the front yard to have a breath of fresh air, and I saw my neighbour Jeffrey in his front yard. He saw me and we said "Good morning" to each other.

Then he said, "My wife knocked on your door yesterday, but you did not come out. We want to do some grocery shopping for you." I was totally surprised by his offer.

I said, "You are so kind. Thank you so much."

Then he said, "I am going grocery shopping this afternoon. Give me your list, and I will buy the groceries for you."

"Thank you. I really appreciate that," I said.

That morning I checked my fridge and made a list for my grocery shopping and put money in a small envelope. I took the envelope and visited my neighbour and gave it to him with thanks.

Then in only one hour, Jeffrey knocked on my door and delivered me a bag of groceries. I was so blessed by that! I truly thanked him and also thanked God who looks after me so well in every situation and in any circumstance.

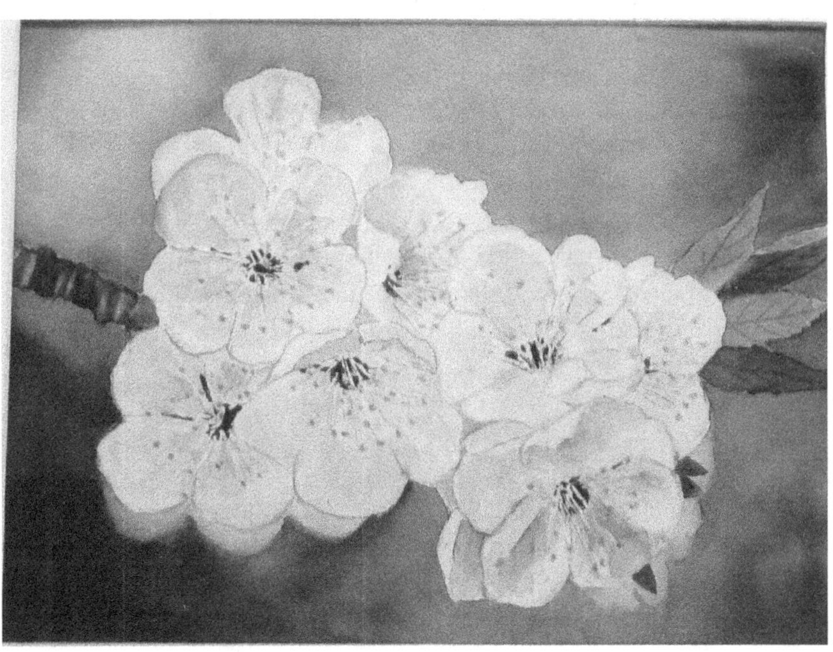

Many of my friends from church called me and offered to do grocery shopping too. Some people live quite a distance from me, yet they offered to do shopping for me. I'm so thankful for being surrounded by very kind people. I truly thanked God for that.

My good friend Daniel and his mother Nan, delivered six packages of homecooked delicious food twice already, and Margaret from our church called me one day, and said "Akemi, I would like to deliver cooked food for you. Give me your address."

I said, "May I ask you why?"

Then she said to me, "Because you are alone, and you are old. I want to help you." I was stunned, and said, "Thank you."

She drove to the front of my house and carried a bag of cooked food to the front door and went to her car and called me. "Akemi, this is Margaret. I put food at your front door."

I opened the entrance door and picked up the bag and saw Margaret in her red car. She was waving her hand. I said, "Thank you" and waved my hand. She drove the car and went to her home. I was totally amazed by her kindness and thanked God who keeps on sending me wonderful friends in my life.

One night my sister, Sanae called me from Japan, and asked me how I was doing by myself in a foreign country. She really worried about me with the coronavirus pandemic. I told her about my neighbours' kind offer to do grocery shopping, and the kind friends who bring cooked food for me. Sanae was shocked by that and said, "I am so glad that you have good friends, and you are looked after well."

"Me too, I'm very thankful for that," I said, and thanked my sister for being concerned about me.

In two weeks, Sanae called me again, and told me about what was happening in Japan. She said that the professional baseball games started without any audience, and also professional sumo started without any audience. She said that was such an empty feeling. Then she said, "You know, you are looked after well in Canada, so we started helping an old lady. She lives by herself on our street, and she is over 80 years of age. So Shigeru and I started grocery shopping for her. She was so pleased, and we are happy too. I don't know why, but here in Japan, people don't care about our neighbours. That's so sad."

"I'm glad to hear that. You are doing a wonderful job," I said. I thanked God in my heart.

A little kindness is repeated in Japan and is making an old lady happy. I believe that that made God happy too. Sanae and I had a good conversation on the phone.

In a time like this, coronavirus is spreading so wide and so fast, and I am so thankful that God's kindness and His love is reaching people's lives and it will spread wider and faster than the virus. I truly hope and pray that many people will come to know the Saviour in this difficult time.

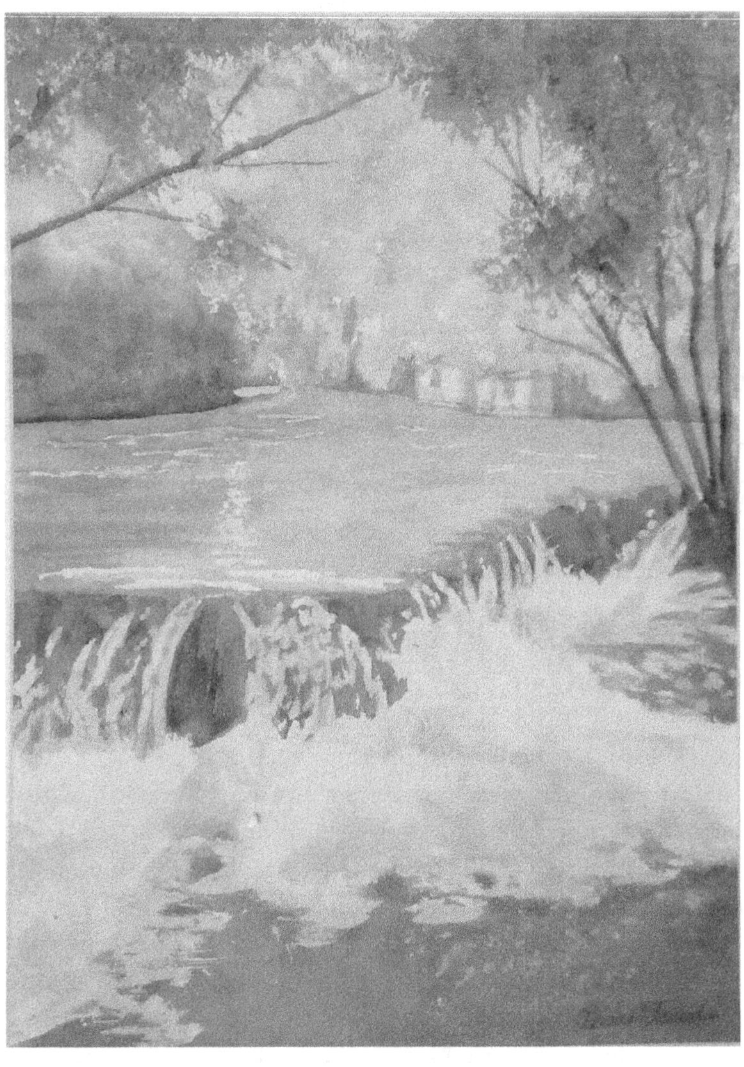

42

I was Alone on Easter Sunday

April 14, 2020

When I woke up on Easter morning, April the 12th, I wondered what kind of day I would have. There was no church service, and no Easter dinner. I was totally alone all day. I never expected an Easter Sunday like this. But I decided to rejoice over the resurrection of Jesus no matter what, because of His resurrection I have life now.

Before I get out of bed, I do exercises on the bed for about 20 minutes. About 10 years ago, I injured my back and visited a chiropractor, and he taught me this exercise for my legs, back and neck. When I finished the exercises on the bed, the telephone rang. It was a long-distance call.

When I said, "Hello," a lady said, "Hello Akemi, this is Ingrid. Happy Easter to you." Ingrid was calling from Germany.

"Happy Easter to you too," I said. I thanked her for her kind call, talked about what is going on in our lives under the coronavirus pandemic. When I said, "It's very difficult. I can't go anywhere, and I am totally homebound."

Then she said, "But Akemi, we have our own houses and gardens. We are so blessed. I thank God for this every day."

That was a good message on Easter morning. I thanked Ingrid and also God. He was speaking to me through Ingrid.

After I talked to Ingrid, I watched Christian TV "Living Truth" from People's Church in Toronto from 9:00 to 9:30 AM. I enjoyed listening to the wonderful message of the resurrection of Jesus through TV.

I went downstairs and prepared an Easter breakfast and ate it. Then I went to the living room and read the Bible, Matthew 28: 1-15, the resurrection of Jesus, and read my devotional book. I enjoy spending time with the Lord by myself as usual. I really enjoyed this quiet time with God. Then I went to the basement to do some radio exercises. My brother-in-law, Shigeru, taped Japanese radio exercises and sent them to me many years ago. Since then, I have been doing this radio exercise every morning for about 15 minutes.

While I was doing this exercise, I heard another telephone call. I ran upstairs and said, "Hello." A lady said, "Hi Akemi, this is Anne."

"Happy Easter to you, Anne," I said.

"Happy Easter to you, Akemi. Would you like to listen to a church service through my phone?"

"I would love to," I replied. "Thank you and, could you give me a couple of minutes to go to the basement and turn off the radio and come upstairs to listen."

"Sure, call me. We will do that," Anne said.

I went to the basement and turned off the tape and went upstairs and opened the Bible and called Anne. Anne put her phone close to her computer, so that I was able to listen to the worship music.

"Can you hear well, Akemi?"

"Yes, I can hear very clearly. Thank you so much. You are so kind," I said.

Anne told me to prepare communion, so I prepared communion.

Because of Anne's kindness, I was able to participate in our own church's Easter service. The worship was so good, and Pastor James Colgan's message was excellent. He emphasized the importance of the resurrection of Christ, and also this resurrected Jesus is living in us now. I was truly thankful for this truth, and also I was able to participate in communion with our church members.

I truly thanked Anne, who gave me a wonderful Easter service. Then Anne said, "When I started watching the Sunday service, your name came to me." I truly thanked Anne and of course a wonderful God.

After I listened to a church service, I went to the basement again, and finished my exercise. As soon as I finished my exercise, I got another call. This time it was my kind hairdresser, Widad. We exchanged "Happy Easter," and talked.

She said, "How are you doing?"

I said, "I am okay, but my hair needs a cut."

"I know your hair is growing." We laughed. I don't know how long

I have to wait, but I strongly desire to visit her hair salon very soon. I truly thanked God for the kind Christian hairdresser He gave me.

After not too long, I had another long-distance call from BC. My husband Ken's co-worker, Irene Csizmadia called me and said, "Akemi, this is Irene. Happy Easter to you."

"Happy Easter to you too. How are you?"

"I am okay, but I had a very busy time, and my son lost his job. He is staying with me now."

She told me about so many things happening in her life. I just listened to her. Irene is a very kind person. She worked with Ken at Atomic Energy Canada Limited for many years, and I did not know her at all, but she started calling me after my husband's death, and when she moved to BC, she connected with me, and I am so thankful for that.

While we were talking, suddenly she said, "You know I really enjoyed working with your husband. He was a good designer, and I wanted to be like him, but I could not. When he became a manager, he wasn't happy, because he could not design anymore."

"Thank you for telling me. I did not know anything about it," I said.

"He enjoyed working with you, Irene," I added.

Irene replied, "Yes, we were a good team. I really enjoyed working for him."

I told her things which I had never told her, "You know Irene, Ken introduced me to art and classical music, and I introduced him to Jesus. He invited Jesus into his life, and his eyes started shining, and only four months later he passed away."

"Oh, that is wonderful. I did not know that."

"Yes, he is in heaven now."

We had a wonderful conversation, and I truly thanked God for a wonderful Easter Sunday.

Very soon, Janis Flowers called me, and we had a good talk about God's bigger plan and His great harvest on earth after a very difficult time.

I thanked Janis who drove me out the day before, because I am alone at this time.

About 3:00 o'clock, I went out to the backyard and started weeding. Perennials were growing, but also weeds were growing too. While I was removing the weeds, my neighbour Jeffrey came out and said,

"How are you doing, Akemi?" he asked me from across the wire fence.

"I am fine. Thank you. Happy Easter to you," I said.

"Happy Easter to you. It's a quiet Easter, isn't it?"

"Yes, it is, just staying home."

"It will come to an end soon," he added.

"I really hope so," I said.

"You know we are going to do grocery shopping on Tuesday. If you need anything, give me a list, okay?"

"Thank you so much. I really appreciate your kindness," I said.

He had helped me with grocery shopping three times already. I am so thankful for his kind help and I thanked God for giving me such a kind neighbour.

Around 6:00 o'clock, Debbie, a co-worker of Gary delivered me a big package of toilet paper, paper towels, and a box of compostable bin liners from Costco. I met her through Gary many years ago, but still she helps me. I truly thanked her for that.

Little after 9:00 o'clock at night, my sister called me from Japan. She said, "Are you still alive?"

"Of course, I am," I said. She told me that coronavirus was hitting Japan so badly, and it's not a comfortable time to live there.

She said, "I sent you a little parcel. I don't know how long it will take. I just hope it will arrive safely."

I truly thanked her for her kindness. She never stops looking after her older sister.

I stayed home by myself on this Easter Sunday, without attending church and Easter dinner, but six people called me and greeted me. Two people helped me to make my life safe. I truly thanked God for His kind help over a little widow. I spent a beautiful Easter and thanked God for the resurrection of His son Jesus.

43

Thank You for the Last 20 Years

May 15, 2020

Spring has come, and the perennials in the garden have started growing. Spring flowers started blooming, and I saw many buds on the branches of the wisteria.

The 27th of May is approaching, the day my husband Ken, moved to heaven 20 years ago. I still remember the day he passed away. It was a beautiful, sunny Saturday morning. The garden Ken completed was so beautiful, and wisteria bloomed for the first time. We expected to enjoy a beautiful garden that year, and suddenly my husband passed away from a massive heart attack.

Since then exactly 20 years have passed. I can't believe I survived and then for the last 20 years by myself in the country. It is truly a miracle that I was able to live my life alone for the last 20 years. When I look back on my life, I know clearly that because of God's kindness, I was able to live my life.

My journey wasn't an easy one. I went through many valleys. I was overwhelmed by sorrows and fears towards my future living without a husband and children and cried out to God.

"Help me, Lord. If you fail to help me, I can't survive." God answered my request so wonderfully. He sustained me and helped me. Without His help, I could not have survived. Even I did not realize He was with me all the time. When I went through a very difficult time and cried and cried, He was with me. When I cried out to God, "Take me home quickly. I don't want to go through the cold winter.' He was with me. It was truly an amazing journey with God. I want to thank God for His faithfulness and His compassion. He never left me. He was with me all the time.

He helped me in so many ways. He sent me so many wonderful people who helped me and so many ways and made my life easier for the last 20 years.

Janis Flowers came when my husband died and helped me a lot. She is still my good friend and my trustee and helps me a lot. In the COVID-19, she drives me out once a week to see how spring is arriving.

Gary Brady, who came into my life one day after my husband's death, and said, "I am your gardener." He still comes even though he has moved to Guelph and cuts my grass faithfully. He has been cutting my grass and helping me in so many ways for the last 20 years. I really thanked him.

Rita Gervais, who prayed with me and encouraged me since my husband died, can't visit me anymore, but we still connect on the phone and encourage each other.

Anita Khan helps me to do grocery shopping once a week in this difficult time. I'm so thankful for her help.

Danielle Hoogsteen's family bring cooked food for me. I'm so surprised and also very thankful for their kindness and delicious food.

My sister Sanae, from Japan still calls me often, and encourages me. She sends me Japanese goods so faithfully. I'm so thankful for that.

I don't have any meetings at my house anymore, but so many sisters in the Lord call me and encourage me.

God surrounded me with many kind people and is showing me His unchanging love for me.

God is with me when I write essays. I started writing essays before my husband's death. I met a wonderful English teacher, Eleanor Sproule, at a ladies Bible study, and she suggested that I could present one essay every time she came. I decided to write about "The Goodness of God in my Life." Since then I could not stop writing essays. I decided to see something good in my life always, instead of difficulty, and it helped me a lot to live my life. God helped me so much that I was able to write about the goodness of God for the last 20 years.

After Eleanor moved to heaven, her husband Keith Sproule, has been checking and correcting my essay. God is so good and he provides wonderful people in my life continually.

I keep on writing my essays and thank God every time I write.

God is with me when I paint with watercolours. My husband introduced me to art and classical music. After his death, I took art classes at Visual Art Mississauga for many years, and I enjoyed painting so much. I don't drive a car anymore, so I don't take a class, but I really enjoy painting at home. I have such a joy in painting and realized that the Holy Spirit is with me and helping me when I paint. I enjoy painting His beautiful creation, landscapes and flowers.

This year, under COVID 19, I have already painted 10 landscapes and eight cards for my friends' birthdays. I enjoy painting at home and listening to peaceful classical music. I'm so thankful that Ken introduced me to art, and God is with me when I paint. It is such a precious time and I enjoy it so much!

I believe I will continue to paint even after I move to heaven. I truly believe I have an art studio in my mansion in heaven.

God is with me when I work in the garden. I started looking after the garden when Ken left. It was so painful to see the beautiful flowers blooming in the garden after his death. I worked very hard to keep the garden clean, and it was very painful and lonely. But the next summer, one Sunday afternoon, the Lord said to me, "Thank you for looking after my garden." Since then I have enjoyed looking after his garden and sensed the presence of God in the garden. Every time I watered; I saw a double rainbow in the garden. I truly enjoyed being with God in His garden. I spent lots of time in the garden and experienced a piece of heaven on earth and truly thanked God for that.

God is with me in so many ways, but the most important thing I experienced was my journey to the Father's heart. That is the best thing that happened in my life. When I came closer to God's heart, he taught me so many things such as to deny myself, empty my desires, my goals, but to choose His desires and His goals instead. He also taught me to ask His will instead of my will. I thought it would be a very difficult life to ask for only His will, but I found more of His love for me instead. How wide and long and high and deep God's love is for me.

I'm so excited to live my life with God. This journey continues to eternity.

This is my 20 years since Ken's death. I wonder how his life is in heaven. He is living an eternal life, so 20 years must be a blink of an eye, but I believe that he has painted lots of beautiful paintings, and also has a gorgeous flower garden in heaven. I would like to see them one day.

I truly thank God for the way he has helped me for the last 20 years and would like to say again, "Thank you Father, you are so good!"

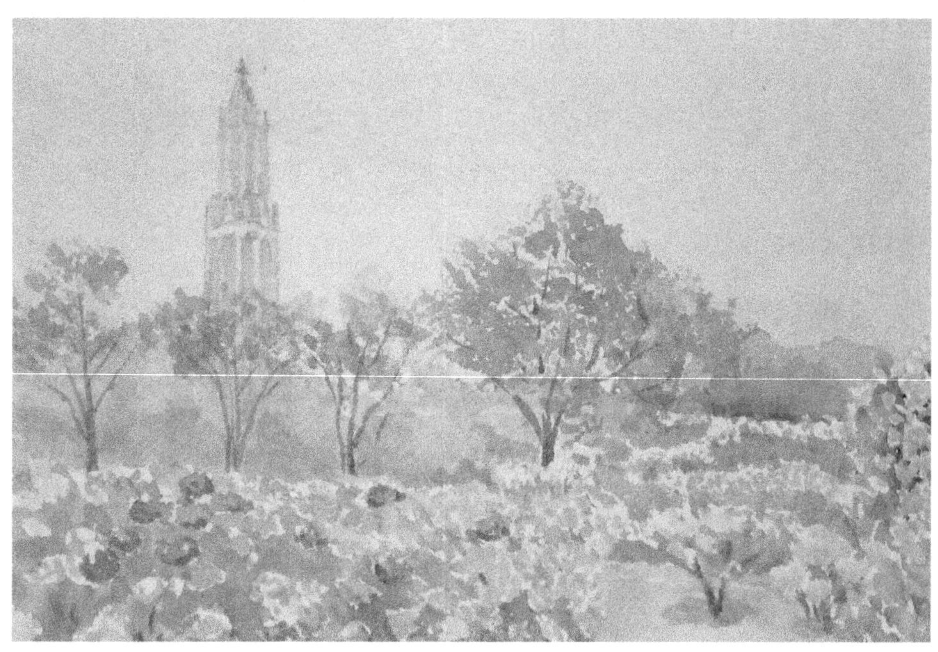

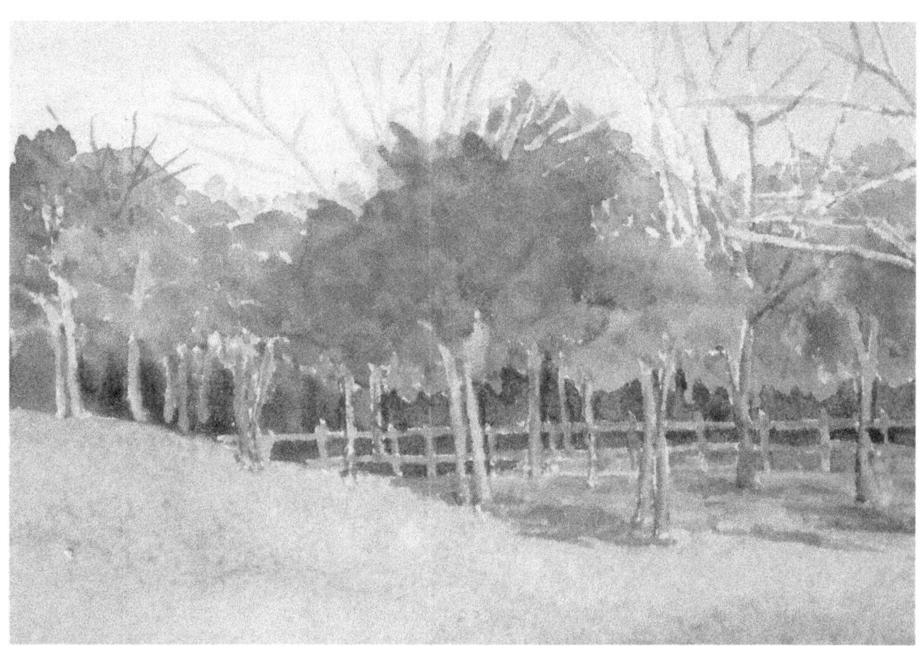

www.ingramcontent.com/pod-product-compliance
Lightning Source LLC
Chambersburg PA
CBHW071309030726
47594CB00002B/361